I Bring You
Good News

Don Baunsgard

ISBN 978-1-64559-887-9 (Paperback)
ISBN 978-1-64559-888-6 (Digital)

Covenant Books, Inc.
11661 Hwy 707
Murrells Inlet, SC 29576
www.covenantbooks.com

To my children, I dedicate this book to you.

Never stop searching, seeking, and running after the truth and love of Jesus Christ and his Word, the Scriptures. For the truth will set you free.

To have imagined, for even a minute, that I would be sitting here writing my second prologue, would be laughable in the least, and completely improbable at best. It is a dream that I never thought possible. So many times, I have been the one on the other side of a book, the reader, wondering how someone could even accomplish such a tedious task as to write a book. This such act qualifies as a perfect example of how God can move within people to inspire within themselves works of talent and gifts unbeknownst to the receiver of such a calling.

It is one of a thousand reasons why I love God so passionately. His love, his truth, and his promises never cease to amaze me, shock me, and propel me into a whole new level of servanthood that continues to fill my heart and soul with so much purpose, goodness, and pure love.

"For I know the plans I have for you, declares the Lord, plans to prosper you, and not to harm you, plans to give you hope and a future. Then you will call on me and come and pray to me, and I will listen to you. You will seek me and find me when you seek me with all of your heart." (Jeremiah 29:11–13)

I have been blessed, once again, from our Savior, with a calling that he has put onto my heart…writing another book.

Back in February of 2018, I began writing my story, *This Thing Called Life*, for the simple reason of relating to my kids the "who, what, and why" of their father, so they need not ask these questions long after I am gone.

The first time that I sat down to write, it took me three months of pouring my heart out into that book and I had not an inkling of what it would take to accomplish such a task. Not to mention, would the contents within it ever be something that (other than my kids) be anything anyone would ever want to read? But of course, once again, I had underestimated the plan that was unfolding, which was what God had planned all along.

I have tried with a humble heart to maintain the reality that I cannot for any reason have any expectations from which to imagine, predict, or forecast how well this book will be received. I simply have to trust God and believe that whatever plan he has for all of this, it would serve his purposes and that is all I needed to know. If either one of my books gives hope or inspiration, or helps even one person on their journey or brings just one more person into a relationship with Jesus, then in my mind, it was a complete success. What I do know from my experience is that God always does amazing and beautiful things when we obediently move as he calls us to do his will. I have already felt and seen with an overwhelming love, the reactions and responses as to how my first book is touching lives, simply because I listened and obeyed his calling that I felt so strongly on my heart.

And now, here I am again, faithfully following the Rabbi, listening to his Word, writing down into my second book all that the Holy Spirit is feeding into me so that God's beautiful works may be answered through his children who love him so.

I have felt for some time now that throughout my own life and my own personal studies of the New Testament for thirty-plus years, there just might be a possibility, that someone else might benefit from what I have found and have then applied to my own life. That through my own journey of discovery, this would be beneficial to those who are searching for answers as I once was so many years ago.

Somewhere, there is someone who is on the fence about this guy, Jesus. Maybe you are a new believer searching for answers. Perhaps you are a lifelong Christ-follower who has been searching to understand for years now the Good News of the New Testament.

Whomever God has brought together, all of us, every single one of us, needs to hear it and apply the Scriptures into our own lives.

God's Word is alive and needs to be taken seriously. It needs to be written on our hearts, and it needs to be a huge part of our lives.

Time is of the essence! Now…not later. We are living in dark times, and if there is anything we need now more than anything, it is God in our life with Jesus at the helm. He is the one thread we should be holding onto with everything we have.

I believe God is trying to reach as many as he can, right here, right now, through his children. And I am scared to think how many are not actually listening, searching and knowing Jesus the way he wants to know you. If you, or anyone you know, is "playing church" or trying to fulfill a "religion," then this book might be a good start in finding out what Jesus *truly* wants from us. I can guarantee you that playing church is **not** what he wants and he is most certainly not fond of religion. I invite you on a journey into *relationship*, to uncover and reveal the beauty and love of what Jesus had planned all along for his followers when he said, "Come, follow me."

I can only hope and pray that you find him within these pages. He will speak to you and the Holy Spirit will move in you when your heart and eyes are opened to his illustrious truth. Jesus is calling us, his children, to be a part of his glorious Kingdom. Find your identity, your purpose, and your life, wrapped up in Him so you can truly live the most incredible life you couldn't possibly imagine.

The Scriptures are alive and breathing the most beautiful and loving words of honesty and genuineness, truth and justice, love and forgiveness. Let them penetrate your life and your heart becoming fully immersed in the Good News of Jesus Christ, which is waiting to be found. It is a journey you will never regret taking. So sit down, grab your cup of coffee, and join me on this journey in search of truth, and the answers to life, as I try, with all my might, with the help of the Holy Spirit to bring you the Good News. Love to all and to God be the glory.

"But my life is worth nothing to me unless I use it for finishing the work assigned me by the Lord Jesus—the work of telling others the Good News about the wonderful grace of God."

—Paul, Acts 20:24

Contents

"Yet what we suffer now is nothing compared to the glory he will reveal to us later. For all creation is waiting eagerly for that future day when God will reveal who his children really are. Against its will, all creation was subjected to God's curse. But with eager hope, the creation looks forward to the day when it will join God's children in glorious freedom from death and decay. For we know that all creation has been groaning as in the pains of childbirth right up to the present time. And we believers also groan, even though we have the Holy Spirit within us as a foretaste of future glory, for we long for our bodies to be released from sin and suffering. We too, wait with eager hope for the day when God will give us our full rights as his adopted children, including the new bodies he has promised us. We were given this hope when we were saved. (If we already have something, we don't need to hope for it. But if we look forward to something we don't yet have, we must wait patiently and confidently.)

—Paul, Romans 8:18–25

Chapter 1

Masks

Be weird. Be random. Because you never know who would love the person you hide.
—*C. S. Lewis*

Let people see Jesus in you even before you tell them.
—*Anonymous*

"Christ is the visible image of the invisible God. He existed before anything was created and is supreme over all creation, for through him God created everything in the heavenly realms and on earth. Everything was created through him and for him. He existed before anything else and he holds all creation together."

—Paul, Colossians 1:15–17

He said, "You become. It takes a long time. That's why it doesn't happen often to people who break easily, or have sharp edges, or who have to be carefully kept. Generally, by the time you are Real, most of your hair has been loved off, and your eyes drop out and you get loose in the joints and very shabby. But these things don't matter at all, because once you are Real you can't be ugly, except to people who don't understand."

—The Velveteen Rabbit

On November 16, 2018, only a month after my first book was finished and on its way to being published, I felt another calling from the Holy Spirit to sit down once again as it became quite obvious he wasn't finished with me yet. As I scribbled down as fast as I could what God had put on my heart to say, literally two months later, I was done. That, of course, was followed by three months of editing, and voila…this book you hold in your hands is the final result of that calling.

If there is anything I have learned throughout this journey of life and in my relationship with Jesus…whatever you may think God is up to or is planning…forget about it. His ways are not our ways and his plans are not our plans. Expect to be amazed by our glorious Creator.

Our part in this incredible story of God's creation is to simply choose to listen and participate. We need to accept, to be compassionate and understanding of each other, not to judge but to love each other and to love God. To listen to the Holy Spirit, obey, and then move.

"What good is it, dear brothers and sisters, if you say you have faith but don't show it by your actions? Can that kind of faith save anyone?" (James 2:14)

We, as believers, who follow and serve the most passionate and loving Savior, Jesus Christ, need to wake up and make our faith active and purposeful. We need to be warriors who will no longer sit on our hands, but will stand up and fight the good fight! The time has come for us to stand up and fight for our spouses, fight for our children, fight for God's Good News! Fight to be strong witnesses for Christ! Let us no longer hide in the shadows, but profess our faith passionately, with love and with action! Let us no longer be ashamed of the Gospel or our relationship to Jesus.

"For I am not ashamed of the Good News about Christ. It is the power of God at work, saving everyone who believes—the Jew first and also the Gentile. This Good News tells us how God makes us right in his sight. This is accomplished from start to finish by faith. As the Scriptures say, "It is through faith that a righteous person has life." (Paul, Romans 1:16–17)

Jesus hid from no one and made himself available to everyone… Everyone!

"For you are all children of God through faith in Christ Jesus. And all who have been united with Christ in baptism have put on Christ, like putting on new clothes. There is no longer Jew or Gentile, slave or free, male and female. For you are all one in Christ Jesus." (Galatians 3:26–28)

We, as followers of Jesus, need to be the voice of those who have no voice. We need to be the hands and feet of Christ to those who need him. It's time to step out and serve others with the love he has manifested in us. Lose your life for the sake of God's Kingdom so you will save it. Make Christ no. 1 in your life, stand up and stay strong! He is our Mighty King and we are his warriors of Love, Truth, Forgiveness, and the Way. Live as though heaven is on earth *right now*, because the time is now, not later! Seek out the lost, the hurting, the broken, and the disheartened. Share this Good News everywhere you go! We should be shouting it out from the mountaintops! Jesus! You are Lord and we love you passionately!

Sadly, though, through many trials, challenges, and the difficulties of life, we allow ourselves to get lost in the shuffle, get frustrated, and then dismiss our mission to follow after Jesus on the journey of becoming more like him. Life has a way of cutting it short, dismantling our joy, and stealing away our passion. It is the ultimate battle of our wills to continually move in the direction of Christ and his love and away from this world. But once we accept Jesus into our hearts and lives, aren't we supposed to grow and transform? Become like foreigners in a strange land who are no longer a part of this world? Or are we?

"Dear friends, I warn you as 'temporary residents and foreigners' to keep away from worldly desires that wage war against your very souls. Be careful to live properly among your unbelieving neighbors. Then even if they accuse you of doing wrong, they will see your honorable behavior, and they will give honor to God when he judges the world." (1 Peter 2:11–12)

Each and every single one of us has to coherently come to a final conclusion. We must decide what we believe to be the truth, the final say, and the last word. What is death, what is truly living, and what is the final outcome of all that we know to be true? What is unconditional love, and why are we truly here?

Throughout this book, I will be on a mission to uncover and hopefully bring to the surface the simplistic beauty of God's Good News into plain view. To prayerfully disclose so much of the love, truth, and wisdom that is buried in its message. Too often, we as believers in Jesus Christ, skim over the Word of God and don't stop to chew on the very personal but deeply embedded message that God has for you and for me. For those of you who are seeking, then I pray this book draws you closer to him, the lover of our souls, our Redeemer, Jesus Christ.

"Then Jesus said, 'Come to me, all of you who are weary and carry heavy burdens, and I will give you rest. Take my yoke upon you. Let me teach you, because I am humble and gentle at heart, and you will find rest for your souls. For my yoke is easy to bear, and the burden I give you is light.'" (Jesus, Matthew 11:28–30)

Let me just say that I am not in any way claiming that I have a perfect system, plan, or schedule as to how to read and understand all of the Good News of the Bible. Throughout my life I have had to lean on God's plan and trust that he would bring to light all that I needed to know.

What I am asking each of you, the readers, to do, is to simply go on this journey with me, together. So we can see what we can find revealing the treasure, truth and the Good News of Jesus Christ with hope and excitement.

But first, will you please join me in prayer?

"Father, I pray you will open the minds and hearts of all that come into contact with this book. Break down the walls of restraint, resistance and ignorance. Unlock the secrets and make known your truths to all who are searching. I am no greater or lesser than the one holding this book in their hands. In your eyes, Lord, we are equally loved and adored. Humble us on this expedition for truth as we explore the Gospels and so much more of the New Testament Scriptures. Reveal to us your mysterious plan, your amazing grace, your never-ending forgiveness and your unconditional love. We love you and are so grateful for all your blessings that you give us every day. Thank you Jesus, for allowing us to be on this journey together for I know you are with us. In his precious name we pray, Amen."

Let's get started shall we?

I think that we can all agree that "Growth is painful. Change is painful. But nothing is more painful than staying stuck somewhere you don't belong."—By Mandy Hale

There comes a time when we all must look in the mirror and be honest with ourselves. No longer hiding behind some false identity, but asking ourselves truthfully and with complete honesty…Who am I? And what have I become?

I believe there has to come a time in everyone's life when we recognize our faults, face our mistakes and claim our sins. It is time to take off the many masks we wear and be real. Be you. And then find a way to forgive yourself, love who you are, and go searching for who you were created to be.

If you haven't figured it out yet…time is running out. Next month when I turn fifty years old, I will have lived through 438,000 hours, 18,250 days, 2,600 weeks, and 600 months!

I do realize and try to remember every day that there are so many people that have been born who never had the pleasure or opportunity to have lived to the ripe old age of fifty. Just in the Vietnam War alone, there were 58,200 US military casualties. The average age of the enlisted from the Vietnam War was only twenty-two. In World War II, it was twenty-six.

To even imagine for a minute how many lives have never had the chance to grow and experience life is unfathomable. In the name of war and disease, hatred, racism, religion and ignorance, there have been too many lives snuffed out far too early before their time. It is of the greatest importance then, that we do not squander life. We cannot spare a single day and say it was worthless. Each minute, each hour and every day is valuable unto its own imagination, wisdom learned and life experienced. Do not waste it or throw it away but embrace it with a tenacity that cannot be denied.

Therefore, rip off the masks that you wear and unveil the truth of who you truly are. It is a desecration to have died without ever taking the chance to truly live. Life is to be experienced and will be filled with great joy, love and romance, but also pain and disappointment. We are creatures who long for love and acceptance yet deny our very selves the opportunity to simply be who we are meant to be.

"And God said 'Love your enemy,' and I obeyed him and loved myself." (Khalil Gibran)

The journey of life either becomes an eccentric adventure filled with daring and courageous choices and outrageous decisions or it simply does not match up to what we dreamed it would be. Life also has a tendency to become monotonous, repetitive, and boring while it slowly fizzes out as the days go by. But this life you have been given is a gift of great importance. You have been created, planned by choice. Life was breathed into your lungs and your brain is functioning and full of intense imagination ready to be poured out and enjoyed. You were uniquely developed in the womb of your mother, one of a kind, and you have a special purpose for being on this planet amongst all the others that are here, living and walking around you. Never ever consider yourself or your life a mistake. God does not make mistakes.

"What makes us human is not our mind but our heart, not our ability to think but our ability to love." (Henry Nouwen)

Over your life, you will determine by the influences of those of your inner circle and of those outside your circle, who and what you believe you truly are. How worthy you are, how smart you are, how funny or how unintelligent you believe you are. The list is endless. Fat, short, ugly, beautiful, mean, tall, loving, depressed, caring, giving, destitute, determined, repulsive, organic, the list goes on. You may believe you are a person of great talents or a failure in everything. Fill in the blank with a title, a name badge, a career choice, your sexual orientation or even an undetermined gender. We are searching for answers, searching for our identity and what we believe truly defines us in this crazy thing we call life.

We base our own judgments of ourselves from the input of those we choose to give that power. It starts with our parents, our siblings, our friends, teachers, coaches, significant others, and co-workers. It is up to you to decide what and who you believe you are and should be. "This is your life…are you who you want to be?" (Switchfoot).

Of course, we are also easily persuaded and become defined in our minds through the manipulation of our circumstances. We become distracted by the casualties of war that life seems to throw our way from within the environment where we are born. Again, this is only by surrendering ourselves to the power we are choosing to give these manipulative situations, people and occasions of the life that surrounds us. What we sometimes fail to realize is…we don't have to be the victims of what life throws at us. We CAN choose to be survivors, victors, and reigning champions of life, if we so choose to be.

In your personal view of yourself, what are the messages you believe and say internally on a regular daily basis? How do you view your life, your relationships and your purpose? Do you struggle to believe that you matter? Do you struggle to understand who you truly are in the challenges of life? It is a necessary part of the process that we are looking and searching to "find" ourselves. To find our niche and our purpose. To be a part of a click of friends that you seem to fit in with and are easily accepted as part of the group. Everyone wants to feel and know that they are loved and accepted. This is one of the most recognized forms of our existence for maintaining happiness, joy, love, health, and balance.

In the Gospel of Luke chapter 19, Jesus comes across a man who is hated and despised by the Jews simply because he is the chief tax collector. In those days, there were Jews who chose their profession to be tax collectors who would collect the tax from the Jews for the Roman Empire. Right off the bat you can see how this would be a career choice that would not sit well with your Jewish brothers and sisters. When you choose to go this route, you are basically choosing to be on the side of the Romans and discarding your Jewish heritage, the culture and all that comes with it, and they viewed him as "unclean." On top of that, most, if not all, of the tax collectors were skimming off the top of the taxes collected to line their own pockets.

Once the amount of taxes that were demanded from the Romans were met, anything after that was pocketed by the tax collector. So if the tax collector wanted to ask for more taxes above the amount that was asked for, he could. This is why most of the tax collectors were rich. Zacchaeus, the chief tax collector, also profited from all the tax collectors under his command. Listen to this incredible story of redemption and acceptance for ALL of us who are broken and in need of a Savior…even Zacchaeus.

"Jesus entered Jericho and made his way through the town. There was a man there named Zacchaeus. He was the chief tax collector in the region, and he had become very rich. He tried to get a look at Jesus, but he was too short to see over the crowd. So he ran ahead and climbed a sycamore-fig tree beside the road, for Jesus was going to pass by.

"When Jesus came by, he looked up at Zacchaeus and called him by name. 'Zacchaeus!' he said. 'Quick, come down! I must be a guest in your home today." (Luke 19:1–5)

I need to stop there for a moment to point out how amazing this must have been for this man, Zacchaeus, to hear Jesus call out his name among all the other people in his vicinity. Jesus knew his name and that alone must have shocked Zacchaeus right out of that tree. To hear this Prophet, this Teacher that everyone is talking about and following, for him to stop, take a moment and call out to this man who is hated by so many, his heart must have dropped into his stomach. And then to have heard…

"I must be a guest in your home today."

Wow…what an honor.

"Zacchaeus quickly climbed down and took Jesus to his house in great excitement and joy. But the people were displeased. 'He has gone to be the guest of a notorious sinner,' they grumbled.

"Meanwhile, Zacchaeus stood before the Lord and said, 'I will give half my wealth to the poor, Lord, and if I have cheated people on their taxes, I will give them back four times as much!'

"Jesus responded, 'Salvation has come to this home today, for this man has shown himself to be a true son of Abraham. For the Son of Man came to seek and save those who are lost.'" (Luke 19:1–10)

Wow…what a deep impression this example leaves on us to the depths of absolute truth and unconditional love Jesus has for us…all of us, even the most wretched. This man, Zacchaeus, was despised and hated to the greatest degree, a traitor, because of his chosen profession, and rightly so. I could also make a pretty good assumption that he was probably mocked for his low stature as well. Notorious for his greed and sin, Jesus reaches down into this man's life, deep into his heart and soul and says…

You are worthy of my love, no matter what!

"For the Son of Man came to seek and save those who are lost." (Luke 19:10)

What an incredible story of redemption, acceptance, love, and friendship.

What I would like for you all to know is that I just heard this story in a sermon from my pastor and I felt that it was so profound that it needed to be inserted into this book somewhere because of the significance of its subject matter. I have read this story before many times and have even sensed the beauty within it, but knew right away that this story had to be highlighted and told again.

Zacchaeus's life was turned upside down that day and in his reaction of being accepted and loved by Jesus he chose to make a radical change in his lifestyle, his giving and the status of his wealth. I have no idea what happened after this to Zacchaeus, or his life choices, if he continued to be a chief tax collector or he decided to leave it all behind to follow Jesus, because it does not share the results of this incredible encounter.

What this story reveals to me clearly is that we all need Jesus… no matter where we are and no matter what we have done. Jesus loves us as we are and not as we should be and Zacchaeus's life abruptly changed when Jesus simply asked him to let him be a part of his life and to be his friend, his guest.

God is revealed in how we treat each other, so please remember that no one is out of the reach of the love and forgiveness of Jesus Christ. And as my pastor so lovingly put it…"My brokenness becomes His message."

Our confidence is attractive to those around us only in the concept of knowing who we are and what we believe ourselves to be. Some people find their gifts or talents early in life and some struggle their whole life looking for it. Some people choose, therefore, to define their life around their natural gifts or talents and use it to their best ability. There is nothing wrong with that as long as it does not become something bigger than themselves or that it ends up replacing your relationship with God and where God stands in your life. We must never allow the talent or gift that you have been given to become your god. And it is through the gifts he has given us that we in turn, give glory back to God and not to ourselves.

We are constantly in a conundrum of keeping our thoughts and feelings of ourselves in check. This is where it gets tricky and we have to be careful and also aware to what conclusion we have come to assume ourselves to be.

What all of us must remember daily, minute by minute, is that we are **all** valuable and quite worthy of all the wonderful qualities that life has to offer. Once we allow the tortures of the world's cruelty to invade our minds and our hearts, then we have let them win and they don't deserve to win…not for one minute. Let me make this abundantly clear to you… ***You are loved and more valuable than you will ever know in the eyes and heart of God.*** Life will chew you up and people will spit you out…leave you for dead. It is up to you and you alone to find that value and worthiness within yourself.

Allow God to penetrate your life, allow him to love you, and help you realize how much you have to offer this world despite what anyone else thinks. You have gifts and talents that you are completely unaware of. Look at me for example. I neither knew that I could be successful in a yard sale (more on that later) or in writing a book, but yet with God's help, within the parameters of our friendship and his leadership, I have been able to do both. I am humbled and honored to be a part of God's plan. God believed in me and helped me believe in myself. And now, I have found purpose for my life through God's love, grace and mercy and because I put him first.

Through this incredible journey of life, we are only limited to what we can achieve or what we believe, by the level of the faith that we attain in ourselves and in God.

We settled into our own home for the first time after moving six times between the ages of five and eleven. It was rather challenging to find myself or to find where I fit in with so much disruption. I was constantly having to make new friends and start over once again. When I moved to North Bend, Washington, in the summer before sixth grade, I was unsure as to how I would be accepted or if I would find any friends who didn't think I was too weird.

Quite honestly, I was extremely weird and I often struggled to fit in. It took some time, like it always does, and eventually I made some new friends, but throughout the next few years, I struggled to understand who I truly wanted to be. What kind of personality traits did I feel best suited me, and how did I want to represent myself?

Each of us along the way has to make these choices. We are a constant work in progress and need directions for our lives.

I eventually figured it out, and by the time I was in high school, I believed I had it all nailed down. Of course, at that age, I knew all I needed to know and life was going to be a breeze. Ha! I would soon find out that was not the case. But in high school, I began building some foundations of what I believed were some very important characteristics and qualities that I had certainly decided were important to attain and to build upon. One of the most important factors and truths that I had learned along the way was that I must choose to love who I am so then in turn, others could then love me. Not in a vain and conceited way but in the way that believes in actions and the power of words.

I also came to a true understanding that whomever I decided to be, I must not and could not allow others to derail me from that belief. In other words, I had to know and realize beforehand that there would be people who are not going to like who I was or the characteristics of who I chose to be and that I just cannot care or worry about what others think about me. If I believe that I am a good person who genuinely loves others but still likes to razz people, have fun and make people laugh…then that is who I am and that is okay! If people chose to make fun of me or if they tried to knock me down, I would just brush them off because I knew that this kind of behavior was usually based from a state of fear, insecurity, or jealousy.

I chose to believe in forming a foundation of trust in myself and believing that my heart was good. Always keeping in mind the importance of seeing everyone as equal and never seeing myself as better than anyone else. Just be me. Love who I am even if there are those who don't.

Now, I am only five feet, six inches tall. Okay, fine, I am actually five feet, five and three-quarter inches tall. So I obviously don't qualify for the tall and bullying type. And even if I did, I don't believe I would have ever gone that route. What I did find out though was that I had eventually developed and learned a few ways to make people laugh. My writing may not show it much, but I love to make people laugh (or at least I used to). I became pretty good at impersonations, making silly faces and just being plain goofy. I chose to love life and seek out the beauty and goodness amongst all the pain and the crap so I could grab ahold of life and make it what I wanted it to be, not what others were trying to impose on me or what they believed I was or should be.

My wife and I laugh a ton at each other, tears streaming down our faces and trying to catch our breath and it is so wonderful. And I do believe I make my own kids laugh a lot at my silliness also. My sense of humor though has lost its touch over the years due to the fact that life is a crazy, hectic challenge and we have to eventually grow up. Maturity, responsibilities, the challenges of life, and family have a way of filling up your life to the point that humor dissipates and the seriousness of our position sets in.

But growing up, I had found a way to bring laughter and joy into the hearts and minds of many I came in contact with. Let's be real, though, I was a broken mess and this was just one way to deal with the brokenness of my young life and find an avenue to self-medicate. I was also a bit on the unruly side. But this is who I wanted to be. You either find a way to bring life and joy into your existence or you choose a slow and boring death. I believe it is up to each of us to figure it out and find a way to seek out the beauty, the laughter and the joy that this life truly brings.

Every single one of us has to make a choice each and every morning how we are going to take on the world. In what view and perception are we going to choose to see all that is around us? Do we see and grasp clearly the blessings of our health and the health of our children or are we only going to see that blessing when it is eventually too late? Are we going to feel the warmth of the sun on our faces or are we going to completely miss the extravagant colors of a glorious sunrise because we have become too consumed by the stresses of life?

Can we for once choose to see and hear the miracle of life in the laughter of a little child? We need to open our eyes so we can fully and deeply understand how truly important life is, especially in the form of a precious baby.

Every life, EVERY life is beautiful, important, and should be treasured and fought for. Choose to believe that everyone deserves to be loved and cherished. That everyone has a purpose here on this planet and that means you, too, also are cherished and have a purpose. All of us are wanderers, searching to find our way in this maze of craziness. I am here to tell you…if you are searching…start your search with choosing to accept Christ into your life, into your heart and into your soul. This is the beginning of a new life and a brand new start. Let *him* define your identity.

"But to all who believed in him and accepted him, he gave the right to become children of God." (John 1:12)

If you have the ability to walk, run and jump…that is a gift, and you are blessed.

If you have the ability to talk, hear, see, and smell…that is a gift, and you are blessed.

If you have been given good health, love and support…that is a gift, and you are blessed.

If you have a bed to sleep in, food in your cupboard, and a roof over your head…that is a gift, and you are blessed.

If you have family and friends that love you and care about you…that is a gift, and you are blessed.

Blessings. Even if you are missing some of these components that I just mentioned, you are still blessed with many blessings. A majority of how you see your world and your surroundings lies in the view of the beholder and in the attitude of your heart. Sometimes you have to force yourself to see the blessings when life is challenging. But it almost always depends on your point of view and how you see your world…positive or negative, good or bad, blessings or curses.

"Blessed are the pure in heart, for they will see God." (Matthew 5:8)

Blessings are all around you and are literally attached to you every day of your life. It is up to each of us to see them, claim them and recognize just how blessed we truly are. Life is consuming, challenging and demanding. Life is also not fair a lot of the time. So many things can be detrimental to your peace and happiness. We have to fight to see the joy and light through the storm of night. It is a struggle, no doubt.

For those without Christ in their life…I seriously don't know how they can handle living without him. I am beyond grateful for my relationship with my Lord and Savior. Without his grace and mercy upon my existence on this journey I would either be in a grave somewhere or sitting in a jail cell contemplating what my life could have been.

Life and all its trials and tribulations take a toll on us. We almost lose ourselves to the demands of responsibility, the demands of our job or career, to the demands of being a father or mother, husband and wife. As a parent or guardian, we are consumed by chores, answering our children's questions, helping with homework, after-school activities and sports. On top of that, we are trying to find energy to satisfy the needs of our spouses and to make sure that their cup is full all without draining our own.

Now throw in a flat tire, changing diapers, your kids vomiting, and bills needing to be paid. Stress-o-rama! Get married, they said… Have children, they said… Buy a house, they said… It will be fun, they said! In all reality, having a family and being in a healthy and thriving relationship with your kids and your spouse is a beautiful thing and a true and wonderful blessing. It is the biggest challenge you will ever undertake in the arena of unselfishness and love.

Being a servant to your kids and to your wife or husband will help you grow in leaps and bounds, especially if you were looking for help in understanding what unselfishness means and how you can apply it to your life. It also means you are going to give a lot of who you are to your family and you may not receive that much in return. Welcome to being a part of the family.

In my utmost opinion, this is where the voice and wisdom of God truly shines in the words of the Good News, our "Life Manual." When you dive into God's word, you will find beautiful wisdom, a wealth of truth and an unwavering example of unconditional love that is represented in the trinity of the Father, the Son, and the Holy Spirit. Trust is hard to find and even harder to come by. Our only hope is in the one true God…and when you understand that, life slowly becomes an easier pill to swallow day by day.

Let me make sure you understand something about me. I have failed and will continue to fail in this thing called life. I fall down every day. I sin and have to repent *every day*. No one on God's green earth is either better or worse than the person standing next to them. Every one of us has quirks, poor choices, and addictions strewn throughout our days. Secrets and bondage to an addiction that we fight against and have trouble finding a way to win. But here is where the beauty goes deep. No matter what you have done or will ever do…God loves you!

Let that sink in to the depths of your soul. Let the truth of God's love penetrate the deepest, darkest and ugliest truths about you that no one else has ever known. Then, allow God to show you the purest source of love. He who sees right through all your crap and says to you, *"I love you no matter what!"* This voice, this calling on your heart is from Jesus. The one who said, while experiencing excruciating pain and brutally fastened to wooden beams, blood dripping and with thick pieces of metal piercing his wrists and feet…

"Father, forgive them, for they know not what they are doing." (Luke 23:34)

Amazing grace from the One who loves us passionately.

The following song, which is so gloriously sung by a talented singer by the name of *Lauren Daigle* is beautifully written and has just the right words to explain God's grace and mercy on our lives. The song explains our struggle with life and trying to understand how God can love us even though we don't deserve it.

> *"You Say"*
> *I keep fighting voices in my mind that say I am not enough.*
> *Every single lie that tells me I will never measure up.*
> *Am I more than just the sum of every high and of every low?*
> *Remind me once again just who I am because I need to know.*
> *Oooh, ohhh…You say I am loved…when I can't feel a thing,*
> *You say I am strong…when I think I am weak.*
> *You say I am held…when I am falling short.*
> *And when I don't belong…oh, you say I am yours.*
> *And I believe, oh, I believe, what you say of me*

I believe
The only thing that matters now is everything you think of me.
In you I find my worth, in you, I find my identity.
Ooh, ohhh, you say I am loved, when I can't feel a thing.
You say I am strong, when I think I am weak.
You say I am held, when I am falling short.
When I don't belong, you say I am yours.
And I believe…oh, I believe…what you say of me
Oh, I believe
Taking all I have and now I'm laying it at your feet.
You'll have every failure God, you'll have every victory.
You say I am loved, when I can't feel a thing.
You say I am strong when I think I am weak.
You say I am held when I am falling short.
When I don't belong, you say I am yours…and I believe, I
*   believe…what you say of me….*

I absolutely love that song so much! So much raw truth.

In the Gospel of Matthew chapter 7, verse 24, Jesus says this:

"Everyone who hears these words of mine and puts them into practice is like a wise man who built his house on the rock."

The truth is…his words, his example, his love and forgiveness, are the only things in this whole world that has given me any hope and stability. I have put my trust, my will, my plans and my story into his hands. I have put my sin, my temptations, and my addictions into his hands and laid them at the foot of the cross. I have had to repeatedly hand over my rejections, my inhibitions, and my negative thoughts at the foot of the cross. Because the truth is…at the foot of the cross is where you will find the pool of blood that Jesus bled, that lay damp and open for us to cleanse our weary souls of all the burdens, sins and addictions we choose to carry with us daily. This is where we have hope, where we can find healing, find forgiveness and start over again. At the foot of the cross of Jesus, we are welcomed with open arms stretched out wide…battered, bruised, bloody, and pierced…saying to us, "Look how much I love you!"

I love you "THIS" much.

On the cross lay the man who proclaimed himself to be the Son of God, the Messiah who was prophesied…the King of the Jews. But on that day, what his disciples, his followers and the Jews saw, was not a king but a defeated man. One who proclaimed salvation but who also prophesied his death on the cross eleven times (documented in the Gospel of Matthew). Not only did Jesus take on his shoulders the sins of the entire human race, but he also wrapped himself up in addiction, slavery, abortion, hatred, racism, pornography, adultery, and every evil thing that we possess, every sin. Three days later, his prophesy of himself resurrected, came true and changed the course of the disciples' lives and quite literally the lives of every human being born then, up until now, and until the end of time.

"He was pierced for our rebellion, crushed for our sins. He was beaten so we could be whole. He was whipped so we could be healed. All of us, like sheep, have strayed away. We have left God's paths to follow our own. Yet the Lord laid on him the sins of us all." (Isaiah 53:5–6)

"*The balance of power shifted more than slightly that day on Calvary, because of who it was that absorbed the evil. If Jesus of Nazareth had been one more innocent victim, like Martin Luther King, Mandela, Havel, and Solzhenitsyn, he would have made his mark in history and faded from the scene. No religion would have sprung up around him. What changed history was the disciples' dawning awareness (it took the Resurrection to convince them) that God himself had chosen the way of weakness. The cross redefines God as One who was willing to relinquish power for the sake of love.*

"*Power, no matter how well-intentioned, tends to cause suffering. Love, being vulnerable, absorbs it. In a point of convergence on a hill called Calvary, God renounced the one for the sake of the other.*" (Philip Yancey, The Jesus I Never Knew)

Our identity over our lives takes on many new faces and many different titles and many different masks. Year after year, our lives change and transform. We continue this chameleon act over and over again looking to find our one true title, uniform, and name badge. Looking to find our purpose and our personality or someone who will love the person we have become. Am I worthy of such love? Am I so broken that I am unlovable?

Our identity is grounded in our beliefs and the one true faith we have sold out for. That faith can be based and grounded in many different facets of life. May it be politics, career, legalistic religion, false religion, the occult, faith in monetary gains, addictions, our wealth, our material things, our kids and the stock market, or even as simple as in our own relationships.

Our identity can be wrapped up in one or in many masks we choose to wear. Sometimes we allow our title to become more important than anything else. We feel empowered by our social status and wealth, our position in our career, then we fall into that trap and we start believing that we are secure in our own choices, decisions, and our financial status. We come to the conclusion that we don't necessarily need a Savior, or to believe in a God that can save us. Who better to save me but from the one who knows me best...Me?!

Then, as soon as tragedy hits...cancer, a car crash that leaves a loved one paralyzed, you lose an unborn child, your house burns down, etc., we then realize that we were not in control after all and we are in desperate need of God! We choose to pray. We ask God for help, crying out to him...help us, save us! When all along you believed you had control. You believed that your foundation was secure. *"I am surely blessed therefore I don't need to spend time with God, I am much too busy for that."* Don't be fooled into believing you are "all good" just because of your comforts, your health, your financial status or your fame. Stay focused on the only one who can give you peace, understanding, and forgiveness. And most of all, eternal life.

I believe that one of the biggest hurdles (for most of us and even those of us who have accepted Christ) is to actually believe that you are loved and that you are a child of God. Our identity is in suffering, for it longs to be that which God wants for us...and that is to be in the likeness of his Son, Jesus.

So many followers of Jesus want very much to know him and to take on the likeness of Christ, a Christian, but lack the ability to know how. Therefore, their inability to accept and to truly know his grace and forgiveness upon their lives is lost in the craziness and consumption of life and all that it has to offer. We choose to allow all that the world wants to offer us instead of embracing and understanding all that God is offering us.

When certain people are praised for their efforts, their title, their good looks or [fill in the blank]…their focus begins to be absorbed by how the world sees them and they respond with pride and conceit. A disconnect between Jesus and the follower becomes a rather wide chasm that is not easily filled in.

We lose touch and understanding of what our true place is in the Christian community and what it truly means. Our time with God and our relationship with him suffers, and we fall into the ways of the world. When our alignment with God is broken or skewed we have a tendency to fall back into our own sinful nature and suffer into the consequences of our sin and poor choices. Which in turn causes a major malfunction and undeserved suffering to those around us who we love and care about most, and then onto ourselves. We bring suffering, pain, guilt, and shame…again and again…believing that we can do this life without Christ.

Let me ask you a couple of simple questions. But first, I want you to think about your Bible. What does your Bible look like? Not the Bible your mom or dad handed down to you…but your own personal Bible? Is it stained with coffee, underlined, and highlighted to no end? Is there writing all over the margins or is it sitting on a shelf collecting dust? Is it filled with stains from your grateful tears within its pages because of the overwhelming truth of his love and mercy on your life? Is it wrinkled and torn with worn marks on its binder and cover? Or is it lost and placed somewhere you haven't a clue, and would not even know where to start looking for it?

This, by the way, is a pretty clear sign as to how much time you spend with God. Your relationship is most likely on fire for Jesus or it is completely nonexistent.

Please consider the importance of your relationship with God. It cannot be lukewarm while you are sitting in pew a couple of Sundays a month and believe you have a good thing going. Throughout the four Gospels of Jesus's life and example, he left with us many insights to what it means to be a follower of him. He made it very clear that if we choose to follow him, and call ourselves Christians, then we must take up our own cross.

"Then Jesus said to his disciples, 'If any of you wants to be my follower you must turn from your selfish ways, take up your cross, and follow me. If you try to hang on to your life, you will lose it. But if you give up your life for my sake, you will save it. And what do you benefit if you gain the whole world but lose your own soul? Is anything worth more than your soul?'" (Jesus, Matthew 16:24–26)

"I would have marveled at Jesus' parables, a form that became his trademark. Writers ever since have admired his skill in communicating profound truth through such everyday stories. A scolding woman wears down the patience of a judge. A king plunges into an ill-planned war. A group of children quarrel in the street. A man is mugged and left for dead by robbers. A single woman who loses a penny acts as if she has lost everything. There are no fanciful creatures and sinuous plots in Jesus' parables; he simply describes the life around him.

"The parables served Jesus' purposes perfectly. Everyone likes a good story, and Jesus' knack for storytelling held the interest of a mostly illiterate society of farmers and fisherman. Since stories are easier to remember than concepts or outlines, the parables also helped preserve his message: years later, as people reflected on what Jesus had taught, his parables came to mind in vivid detail. It is one thing to talk in abstract terms about the infinite, boundless love of God. It is quite another to tell of a man who lays down his life for his friends, or of a heartsick father who scans the horizon every night for some sign of a wayward son.

"Jesus came to earth 'full of grace and truth,' says the gospel of John, and that phrase makes a good summary of his message. First, grace: in contrast to those who tried to complicate the faith and petrify it with legalism, Jesus preached a simple message of God's love. For no reason—certainly not because we deserve it—God has decided to extend to us love that comes free of charge, no strings attached, 'on the house.'" (Philip Yancey, *The Jesus I Never Knew*)

The book I just quoted, *The Jesus I Never Knew*, is easily one of my all-time favorite books. I have read it at least four times and every time, at the end of that book, I am bawling, because of the overwhelming truth and love that is displayed so clearly in the words and life of *Philip Yancey.*

We, as followers of Christ, are constantly challenged to find our identity in him and him alone. Because we are all broken and sinful, we must start the process of trust and belief in the One and only Son of God. But to trust and believe, you must invest your time into getting to know the one who gave his life as a ransom for your soul. He patiently waits for all of us to turn our gaze to the heavens and cry out to him in praise and in pain so he can comfort us, love us, wrap his arms around us so we know that everything is going to be alright. When we don't draw near to him we suffer greatly at the hands of our own choices and decisions. Choose to lay down your inhibitions, selfishness, and pride so he can envelop you with his overwhelming love and forgiveness. Choose to humble yourself before the Lord. Choose to surrender your life to him.

This is where the road to faith begins. This is where the journey starts and the love of Jesus, his forgiveness, and his grace, will start the painful process of ripping off all the masks that you have been wearing for far too long. He will strip you of your costume and you will be set free from your past to enjoy the freedom of no longer being condemned. Then you will be able to allow yourself to find your true identity in Christ and in your relationship with him. God's word and his love will penetrate your soul, he will reveal the darkness that needs to be removed and shed light into your heart and then, your life will never be the same again. The only mask that people will see, which is no mask at all, will be the light of God's love shining out the door of your heart and the windows of your eyes revealing all that God sees so that you will know and understand his mysterious plan.

"Here at the cross is the man who loves his enemies, the man whose righteousness is greater than the Pharisees, who being rich became poor, who gives his robe to those who took his cloak, who prays for those who despitefully use him. The cross is not a detour or a hurdle on the way to the kingdom, nor is it even the way to the kingdom, it is the kingdom come." (John Howard Yoder)

Chapter 2

Love of Scripture

"Pilate said, 'So you are a king?'
    Jesus responded, 'You say I am a king.
Actually, I was born and came into the world
to testify to the truth. All who love the truth
recognize that what I say is true.'"

                                    —John 18:37

"Therefore, since we are surrounded by such a huge crowd of witnesses to the life of faith, let us strip off every weight that slows us down, especially the sin that so easily trips us up. And let us run with endurance the race that God has set before us. We do this by keeping our eyes on Jesus, the Champion who initiates and perfects our faith. Because of the joy awaiting him, he endured the cross, disregarding its shame. Now he is seated in the place of honor beside God's throne."

—Hebrews 12:1

A couple of years ago, I came up with an idea to do something radically different and really cool with the Scriptures of the New Testament. I decided that I would go line by line from the Gospel of Matthew all the way through the entire New Testament to the end of Revelation and find specific words or titles that I could mark with a certain symbol and then count those symbols to see how many times they had been written or said. I would be searching for words that are repetitive and have substantial meaning in the stories being told like love, sin, faith, God, and the many names of Christ.

Now, I knew that I was initially going after certain words and titles, but along the way, I found so many more that kept popping up that I decided I had to try and keep track of all that I could find.

So after a couple months or so, I painstakingly worked my way through verse by verse and book by book, looking for only these words, quotations, or names that were either repeatedly being used or a theme that was purposefully being integrated so as to make a serious point or expose an obvious truth. After all that was said and done, Jesus and God, and most rightly so, were mentioned far more than anything else that I eventually located throughout the New Testament Scriptures.

But before I continue, I will have to make an assumption that there is a good chance that my numbers in the counting process may be off by a few. I also want to clarify that not once did I cheat by using the internet or any other sources. Everything I found was from my very own Bible.

Just to be sure, there could be a few variations when choosing what translation of the New Testament you are reading. I pursued this fun exercise with the New Living Translation Bible. With that being said…can I get a drum roll, please?

The winner of the most words or names mentioned in the entire New Testament is…God. No surprise there. God was mentioned from Matthew to Revelation 1,909 times and that is not even including all the other names that were used to describe or mention our Father in heaven. In second place was Jesus Christ at 1,839 times. A difference of only about seventy times. Here is the rest of the list from highest to lowest:

Lord: 629
Sin/sins/sinner/sinful nature: 367
Faith: 312
Love/loving/love one another: 289
Holy Spirit: 278
Father: 262
Heaven: 190
Pray/Prayer: 157
Believe/believe in Him/believed: 149
Scriptures: 136
The Good News: 126
Believers: 116
Son: 112
Cross/crucify/crucified/Blood of Jesus/sacrifice: 112
Heal/healed: 108 (only said in the Gospels and Book of Acts)
Kingdom/Kingdom of Heaven/Kingdom of God/ Kingdom of Christ: 103
Son of Man: 89
Grace: 89

Messiah: 87 (only said or used in the Gospels and the Book of Acts)

The Message/Gospel Message: 86

Glory/glorious/eternal glory; 86

Forgive/forgiven/forgiveness: 75

Save/saved/saving/saved us: 70

Peace: 69

Holy: 66

The quote from Jesus in all four Gospels, "I tell you the truth": 64

Mercy/merciful: 61

Righteous/righteousness: 60

The Truth: 58

Bless/blessed/blessings: 55 (only in the Gospels and Book of Acts)

Suffering/suffered/suffer: 51

Salvation: 50

Eternal life/everlasting life: 50

Wisdom: 50

Doing good/do good things/good deeds: 47

Word of God: 47

The quote from Paul in five different books, "Makes us right with God"/"Made right with God": 46

Obey/obedient: 46 (27 of which were in the Book of Romans)

Joy/rejoice: 43

Teacher: 39

Son of God: 35

Light/Light of the world: 35

Christians: 30

The quote "Scriptures says": 29

Humble: 23

Hope: 18

There were quite a few others that I had been watching and keeping track of such as Rabbi, Master, Prophet, Son of David, Shepherd, and I Am. All ending in the seven to fourteen range. What I did find, which I thought was really fascinating, was how many different titles and names that had been used or given to Jesus throughout the New Testament to describe the Son of God. I found eighty-one different names or titles that the authors had used. I am sure there are more than this and that I probably missed a few but sit back and read all the names that I did find:

Jesus, Christ, Messiah, Lord, Teacher, Rabbi, Immanuel, God, Son of God, Son of Man, Son, Shepherd, Good Shepherd, Servant, Hope, Beloved, Prophet, King, King of the Jews, Son of David, Master, Stone, Cornerstone, Rock, Holy One, I Am, King of Israel, Savior, Light, Chosen One, Holy One of God, Word, Unique One, Lamb of God, Stairway between Heaven and Hell, Bread of Life, The Gate, The Resurrection and The Life, I Am the Way, the Truth and the Life, True Grapevine/Vine, Author of Life, Prince, Righteous One, Passover Lamb, Word of Life, The Truth, The Man, Mediator, O' God, God's Messenger, High Priest, Creator, New Covenant, Good News, Coming One, The Champion, The One, Great Shepherd, Guardian of your Soul, The Morning Star, Eternal Life, Advocate, Sacrifice, Son of the Father, Faithful Witness, Alpha and Omega, Light of the World, The First and the Last, The Living One, Amen, The Lion of the Tribe of Judah, The Lamb, The Lord of Lords, King of Kings, O Holy One, True, Word of God, The Beginning and the End, The Bright Morning Star and finally, The Message.

While some of these names were only used once, others were repeated throughout the twenty-seven books of the New Testament. To have found all these different descriptions and names was truly a sight to behold and a true testament to the impact that Jesus had made on his disciples and his followers. With the descriptions and immense information being handed down from one eye witness to the next, this was certainly no ordinary man.

I found many themes and subject titles across each book of the New Testament that always circulated around the life, the message, the love, the example and the sacrifice of Jesus Christ. In fact, the whole Bible is about Jesus and the love story of redemption to bring us back into a relationship with the Father which was lost in the Garden of Eden.

The Holy Bible was written over a span of 1,600 years, across three continents, Africa, Asia, and Europe, by over forty authors in three languages: Aramaic, Hebrew, and Greek. Yet it has only ONE primary theme: Jesus, the Son of God!

"For you know that God paid a ransom to save you from the empty life you inherited from your ancestors. And the ransom he paid was not mere gold and silver. It was the precious blood of Christ, the sinless, spotless Lamb of God. God chose him as your ransom long before the world began, but he has now revealed him to you in these last days.

"Through Christ you have come to trust in God. And you have placed your faith and hope in God because he raised Christ from the dead and gave him great glory.

"You were cleansed from your sins when you obeyed the truth, so now you must show sincere love to each other as brothers and sisters. Love each other deeply with all your heart.

"For you have been born again, but not to a life that will quickly end. Your new life will last forever because it comes from the eternal, living word of God." (1 Peter 1:18–23)

What was it that had sparked so much interest and excitement in these men and women to go so far as to put their very lives on the line between life and death just because of their faith? It seems as if something extraordinary, monumental and miraculous must have taken place for the lives of so many people to begin a church that was spreading like wild fire from the hills of Jerusalem all the way to Rome and to the rest of the world. All the while, their Christian brothers and sisters were being hunted down, set on fire and being used as human torches in the streets of Rome.

Rejoicing in their belief of the risen Christ and choosing to be followers of "the Way," they followed a man who was crucified for claiming he was the coming Messiah. Jesus claimed that he was wisdom personified and that he was the one by whom God will judge all humanity, whether they confess him or dismiss him.

"John the Baptist, who was in prison, heard about all the things the Messiah was doing. So he sent his disciples to ask Jesus, 'Are you the Messiah we've been expecting, or should we keep looking for someone else?'

"Jesus told them, 'Go back to John and tell him what you have heard and seen—the blind see, the lame walk, the lepers are cured, the deaf hear, the dead are raised to life, and the Good News is being preached to the poor. And tell him, God blesses those who do not turn away because of me.'" (Matthew 11:2–6)

After it was all said and done, taking the time to scan the Scriptures word by word and find all that I could find was a very cool exercise and a ton of fun to do. It was also an incredible way to learn about God's Word and find things in it you may have never seen before. If you haven't already figured it out…I LOVE the Scriptures. They fascinate me to no end. The Scriptures are to me the building blocks of life. They open up the phone lines of communication with God.

For me, they provide the hope that decreases stress; they give me a channel with which I can tune in to find the answers to the overbearing struggles of life. They help to minimize and separate all the garbage and the balderdash of what the world emphasizes and simplifies it so that it is far easier to understand and manage.

I love them because it changes the whole game of life and centralizes all of the most important components that we need to focus on to build our faith. It is the very essence of truth, love, faith, mercy, forgiveness and sacrifice. The Bible, the Scriptures and especially the New Testament, is a love story about the greatest super hero that ever came into our existence and is still right here among us, in the hearts of millions, if not billions, in the man-God of Jesus Christ.

The baby Messiah, conceived by the power of the Holy Spirit, was born miraculously from a virgin over two thousand years ago. He came into the world, the Son of God in human flesh, vulnerable and as weak as any other baby. The angel, Gabriel, visited Mary and Joseph and told them to name the baby Jesus, and like any other baby, this baby needed to be coddled, fed, and bathed, raised like any other child.

"She will bear a Son; and you shall call his name Jesus, for he will save his people from their sins." (Matthew 1:21)

Our Savior, who chose to lower himself to a baby boy lying in a manger, was not born of Kings, but born in a small town called Bethlehem to a poor Jewish couple in the royal line of David. The prophesy was foretold from the prophet Micah, which took place seven hundred years before Jesus made his glorious appearance into the world.

"But you, O Bethlehem, are only a small village among all the people of Judah. Yet a ruler of Israel will come from you, one whose origins are from the distant past. The people of Israel will be abandoned to their enemies until the woman in labor gives birth. Then at last his fellow countrymen will return from exile to their own land. And he will stand to lead his flock with the Lord's strength, in the majesty of the name of the Lord his God. Then his people will live there undisturbed, for he will be highly honored around the world. And he will be the source of peace." (Micah 5:2–5)

In the Gospels of Matthew and Luke, the prophecy mentioned in Micah was fulfilled in their descriptions telling of the birth story and the little town of Bethlehem.

"And there were shepherds living out in the fields nearby, keeping watch over their flocks at night. An angel of the Lord appeared to them, and the glory of the Lord shone around them, and they were terrified. But the angel said to them, 'Do not be afraid. I bring you good news that will cause great joy for all the people. Today in the town of David a Savior has been born to you; he is the Messiah, the Lord. And this will be a sign to you: You will find a baby wrapped snugly in strips of cloth, lying in a manger.'

"Suddenly a great company of the heavenly host appeared with the angel, praising God and saying,

"'Glory to God in the highest heaven, and peace on earth to those with whom God is pleased.'

"When the angels had returned to heaven, the shepherds said to each other, 'Let's go to Bethlehem! Let's see this thing that has happened, which the Lord has told us about.'

"They hurried to the village and found Mary and Joseph. And there was the baby, lying in the manger. After seeing him, the shepherds told everyone what had happened and what the angel had said to them about this child. All who heard the shepherd's story were astonished, but Mary treasured all these things in her heart and thought about them often. The shepherds went back to their flocks, glorifying and praising God for all they had heard and seen. It was just as the angel had told them." (Luke 2:8–20)

Did you know that a donkey is the only animal in the world with a cross on its back? Mary rode into Bethlehem on a donkey all the way from Galilee to give birth to Jesus. Then, around thirty years later, Jesus rode on a donkey into Jerusalem where he was eventually arrested and sentenced to die.

To say you believe in the Christmas story is to have been touched in a very deep and intimate way by our Savior. Every Christmas morning, it has been our family tradition to read the birth of Jesus from the Gospel of Luke chapter 2. It is easily my favorite tradition at Christmas time. Jesus is truly the reason for the season.

Right this very minute as I am jotting this chapter down, I am drinking egg nog and preparing for Christmas 2018. And every year I have to remind myself that Christmas is not about presents and Santa Claus, a tree adorned with lights, Christmas cards and ornaments. It is not about covering our homes and shrubbery in decorated twinkling lights or putting decorations on our lawns. It is about the most amazing event that has ever happened in the history of our world and our existence since the beginning of creation. A choice that involved a love so deep for us, that God gave his only Son up for adoption knowing full well that eventually his Son would be sacrificed to the depths of evil by the darkness and cruelty of humanity.

He was sent to earth in the form of a helpless baby boy, born in the poorest conditions in a dirty loft amongst animals, a manger as a bed made of a trough filled with hay and wrapped in strips of cloth. The God of the universe didn't proclaim the entry of his Son, the Savior, into the world to wealthy merchants or to Kings and Queens…but to the lowest and poorest people in that region…the shepherds. They were the ones chosen to not only be a witness to the angels singing…

"Glory to God in the highest and peace on earth to those with whom God is pleased!" (Luke 2:14)

But also to go and find the baby Jesus and tell his parents what they heard and what they had been blessed to have seen.

How ironic, that God chose them above all others to exclaim to everyone the birth of our Messiah, born in a small podunk town called Bethlehem. But this is how God works.

Consider, for a moment, how Jesus chose to appear to his followers and his disciples after he rose from the dead, which, by the way, would have been so incredibly rewarding and simply amazing to have been a witness to such a powerful moment in time.

But what if, and just imagine if you will for a minute, if Jesus instead had chosen to reveal himself alive and well to the Pharisees and religious rulers first, with their bewildered expressions of shock on their faces seeing him standing in their presence, after demanding his death and watching him die on the cross…but no!

When Jesus rolled away the stone to make himself known to be alive, he didn't approach the twelve disciples first, or Pontius Pilate or even the Sanhedrin. He first revealed himself alive again to Mary Magdalene, one of his most faithful followers who was, in the eyes of most of the Jewish nation at that time, a sinner, unclean and despised. Not only was she a woman, but a woman with a very dark past as a prostitute. Jewish women in those days were treated like second class citizens and were not even allowed to testify in court, nor was their testimony to be used in any circumstances whatsoever.

But this woman, who proved her love and dedication to Jesus by washing his feet with her tears and drying them off with her hair, knew that Jesus was so much more than just a man. When Jesus had risen from the dead, he told her to go and tell his disciples that he had risen. Jesus chose to have as his witness of his Resurrection, a woman with a tainted past, society's lowest, but none the less, one of his chosen children whom he loved and cherished.

So here we are. We have the shepherds as witnesses at the beginning of the birth of Christ and again, at Jesus rising from the dead, we have a woman giving testimony of this truth. I love the irony in this fact alone. It is not by choice that we hear this story from people in high regard or even from men, which would have strengthened this story and made it more valid. But instead, God chose to go a different route. I love it.

At the very beginning of Luke in the introduction it says:

"Many people have set out to write accounts about the events that have been fulfilled among us. They used the eyewitness reports circulating among us from the early disciples. Having carefully investigated everything from the beginning, I also have decided to write a careful account for you most honorable Theophilus, so you can be certain of the truth of everything you were taught." (Luke 1:1–4)

I have never heard who Theophilus is, but Luke, who really was a historian, a companion of Paul's throughout some of his missionary work and sort of a first-century journalist, decided that the full story of Jesus needed to be investigated and the truth unearthed so as to write his own thorough account of the events that surely took place in the life and words of Jesus of Nazareth.

When I think about the ramifications of what Luke had to go through to get the full story, with all the details, the geographic layout and to make sure he had all the names of the people involved, this certainly was no easy task. I can't imagine how many interviews must have taken place to make sure he quoted Jesus with precise harmony and absolute accuracy. And furthermore, how did Luke keep track of all the information so as to get it all down to eventually put it into a book with twenty-four chapters? There was no tape recorder or paper and pen. Writing on papyrus could not have been an easy task.

Whatever the case, he did it with a tenacity of *Sherlock Holmes*. Not leaving any stone unturned. Luke was not an Apostle of Jesus but definitely a believer, a disciple and a follower. A true Christian.

He ended up witnessing, journaling and writing down all the events of the Book of Acts as well.

"In my first book I told you, Theophilus, about everything Jesus began to do and teach until the day he was taken up to heaven after giving his chosen apostles further instructions through the Holy Spirit. During the forty days after his crucifixion, he appeared to the apostles from time to time, and he proved to them in many ways that he was actually alive. And he talked to them about the Kingdom of God.

"Once when he was eating with them, he commanded them, 'Do not leave Jerusalem until the Father sends you the gift he promised, as I told you before. John baptized with water, but in just a few days you will be baptized with the Holy Spirit.'

"So when the apostles were with Jesus, they kept asking him, 'Lord, has the time come for you to free Israel and restore our kingdom?'

"He replied, 'The Father alone has the authority to set those dates and times, and they are not for you to know. But you will receive power when the Holy Spirit comes upon you. And you will be my witnesses, telling people about me everywhere—in Jerusalem, throughout Judea, in Samaria, and to the ends of the earth.'" (Luke, Acts 1:1–8)

With all the information that is out there, and all the books ever written over the course of two thousand years, no other person on the face of the planet has been written about more than the historical figure of Jesus Christ. Yes, even now, as I am sitting here writing my second book on my experience and relationship with Jesus, I am only adding to the list of books that are available. I do believe without a doubt that no one has changed and or affected more lives in the way that he has.

I, myself, am just one more testimony, one more story of his miraculous love and life transforming forgiveness. This gift is attainable by anyone seeking his love. No one is exempt from his forgiveness, no matter what you've done or how dark your past is! This is simply amazing grace…how sweet the sound!

"Imitate God, therefore, in everything you do, because you are his dear children. Live a life filled with love, following the example of Christ. He loved us and offered himself as a sacrifice for us, a pleasing aroma to God.

"Let there be no sexual immorality, impurity, or greed among you. Such sins have no place among God's people. Obscene stories, foolish talk, and coarse jokes—these are not for you. Instead, let there be thankfulness to God. You can be sure that no immoral, impure, or greedy person will inherit the Kingdom of Christ and of God. For a greedy person is an idolater, worshiping the things of this world.

"Don't be fooled by those who try to excuse these sins, for the anger of God will fall on all who disobey him. Don't participate in the things these people do. For once you were full of darkness, but now you have light from the Lord. So live as people of light! For this light within you produces only what is good and right and true.

"Carefully determine what pleases the Lord. Take no part in the worthless deeds of evil and darkness; instead, expose them. It is shameful even to talk about the things that ungodly people do in secret. But their evil intentions will be exposed when the light shines on them, for the light makes everything visible." (Ephesians 5:1–14)

"May our hearts be ever tender to the wonder of the story, when our God came near to save us, leaving heaven's perfect glory…as a baby in a manger, on a silent starry night, to a world so lost in darkness Jesus Christ became our Light."

(Taken from a Christmas card we were given this year, 2018.)

Throughout my studies and throughout the writings of my books, I have had to Google many different things so as to accurately find the answers I was looking for and to make sure the words I was choosing were accurate to what it is I was trying to say.

This morning as I was lying in my warm bed, not wanting to get up, I started thinking about Old Testament Scripture and I began to wonder how many times Old Testament Scripture was actually mentioned or quoted in the entire New Testament? The final numbers are eye opening but shouldn't be too surprising either. The answer: *855 times!* I was further surprised by how many times the Old Testament Scriptures are mentioned in each book of the New Testament. For example, in Matthew, they are mentioned 96 times. In the Gospel of John, 40. In the book of Romans, 74 times. But in the book of Revelation, which has the most, 249 times! Wow, that is incredible.

I was also curious to find out how many times Jesus quoted the Old Testament. According to Google, here are the results: Jesus quoted the Old Testament approximately seventy-eight times. He referred to the Old Testament as "The Scriptures," "the Word of God," and "the wisdom of God," and it looks like Jesus quoted from twenty-four different Old Testament books. The Scriptures give a record of Jesus quoting from every book of the Pentateuch, the first five books of the Bible, and eight of God's prophets. The Book of Psalms and its words were quoted more often by Jesus than the words from any other book of the Old Testament. Here is some information that I discovered on the internet that I found rather intriguing:

"Jesus knew the Hebrew Scriptures well. While He quoted most often from the book of Psalms, He also quoted from many other books. Deuteronomy comes in second for the book most often quoted, with Isaiah and Exodus ranking third and fourth respectively."

The Prophets that Jesus quoted the writings from consist of Isaiah, Jeremiah, Daniel, Hosea, Jonah, Micah, Zechariah and Malachi.

"Isaiah has often been called 'the evangelical prophet' because he says more about the coming of the Messiah and the redemptive work of Jesus than any other book of the Old Testament. Consequently, there are many important and favorite passages in this book, and it was clearly a favorite of Jesus as evidenced when…

- *He explained his reason for using parables to teach (Isaiah 6:9–10, Matthew 13:14–15, Mark 4:12, Luke 8:10)*
- *He rebuked the Pharisees and scribes for their lip service to God (Isaiah 29:13, Matthew 15:8–9, Mark 7:6–7)*

- *He cleansed the temple by overturning the tables of the money changers (Isaiah 56:7, Matthew 21:13, Mark 11:17, Luke 19:46)*
- *He told the parable of the vineyard (Isaiah 5:1, Matthew 21:33, Mark 12:1, Luke 20:9)*
- *He told the purpose of His earthly ministry (Isaiah 61:1–2, Matthew 11:5, Luke 4:18–19, 7–22)*
- *He told the works He was doing (Isaiah 35:5–6, Luke 7:22)*
- *He told the beginning of sorrows (Isaiah 34:4, Luke 21:26)*
- *He told of cosmic changes in end times (Isaiah 13:10, Matthew 24:29, Mark 13:24–25)*
- *He told of his death (Isaiah 53:12, Luke 22:37)*
- *He told that his ministry will draw people to Him (Isaiah 54:13, John 6:45)*
- *He told that salvation had come to them (Isaiah 62:11, Matthew 21:5)*

Jesus quotes Isaiah to highlight the disconnect between God and the people, but he also quoted Isaiah to remind people of the comfort God will bring through Him as the Lamb of God and the reigning King.

A lesson for all of us…

- *Jesus was quick to wield His Sword, which is the Word of God (Ephesians 6:17, Hebrews 4:12)*
- *Jesus was able to answer questions posed to Him with, "It is written" because He knew God's Word*
- *Jesus was strengthened and empowered by God's Word to face any situation, including death on the cross*

The question for all of us is, do we know the Word of God well enough to quickly recall it in any situation? Do we hide His Word in our hearts and allow it to fill our minds and direct our words and actions?

Commit to start reading your Bible, or to start reading it more often. We speak to God when we pray, but He speaks to us more directly and most clearly when we read His Word. The more we read, the more we learn about Jesus and His will and ways, His purpose and plan for our *lives. Commit, today, to learn God's truths so you can be ready always to give an answer that begins with 'It is written…'" (Shari Abbott, Reasons for Hope *Jesus)*

The Old Testament, in hundreds of places, predicted the prophetical events of the New Testament, and as the New Testament is the fulfillment of, and testifies to, the genuineness and authenticity of the Old Testament, both Testaments must be considered together as the Word of God.

My favorite time of the day is early morning, with a hot cup of coffee, the sunrise beaming through my back window and God's Word, sitting open, ready for me to dive in and find so much to chew on and digest. I have been amazed, surprised, and filled up with so much jaw-dropping information and truth from God's Word that it continues to flood my heart and soul with the purity and freshness of his loving words. Finding books to read that confirm my faith through extensive investigation, comprehensive journaling and detailed archaeology are a continuous shock to the system providing a never-ending array of truth and confirmation to the accuracy and authenticity of the Bible.

It is simply a perfectly preserved ancient historical document of Jewish history that also matches up to the secular history of that timeframe in other ancient writings as well. Consider the evidence:

Evidence from Tacitus

"Although there is overwhelming evidence that the New Testament is an accurate and trustworthy historical document, many people are still reluctant to believe what it says unless there is also some independent, non-biblical testimony that corroborates its statements. Let's begin our inquiry with a passage that historian Edwin Yamauchi calls 'probably the most important reference to Jesus outside the New Testament.'

Reporting on Emperor Nero's decision to blame the Christians for the fire that destroyed Rome in A.D. 64, the Roman historian Tacitus wrote:

'Nero fastened the guilt…on a class hated for their abominations, called Christians by the populace. **Christus**, from whom the name had its origin, suffered the extreme penalty during the reign of Tiberius at the hands of Pontius Pilatus, and a most mischievous superstition, thus checked for the moment, again broke out not only in Judea, the first source of the evil, but even in Rome…'

"*What all can we learn from this ancient (and rather unsympathetic) reference to Jesus and the early Christians? Notice, first, that Tacitus reports Christians derived their name from a historical person called Christus (from the Latin), or Christ. He is said to have 'suffered the extreme penalty,' obviously alluding to the Roman method of execution known as crucifixion. This is said to have occurred during the reign of Tiberius and by the sentence of Pontius Pilate. This confirms much of what the Gospels tell us about the death of Jesus.*

"*But what are we to make of Tacitus' rather enigmatic statement that Christ's death briefly checked 'a most mischievous superstition,' which subsequently arose not only in Judea, but also in Rome? One historian suggests that Tacitus is here 'bearing indirect…testimony to the conviction of the early church that the Christ who had been crucified had risen from the grave.'*

"*While this interpretation is admittedly speculative, it does help explain the otherwise bizarre occurrence of a rapidly growing religion based on the worship of a man who had been crucified as a criminal. How else might one explain that?*" (Michael Gleghorn, *Probe for Answers*)

There are many other ancient sources to investigate. Here is a list for you to look into and find out for yourself how much is accurately backed up that matches and confirms the accuracy, authenticity, and historicity of the New Testament. I hope you take the time to put on your own deerstalker hat (the hat *Sherlock Holmes* wore), put a pipe in your mouth and go to work finding all the clues that lead you to the truth.

- Letters from Pliny the Younger to Emperor Trajan. AD 112
- *Jewish Antiquities*, the writings of Josephus, a first-century Jewish Historian
- Babylonian Talmud, a collection of Jewish rabbinical writings compiled between AD 70–200
- And of course…the Old Testament (look up Isaiah 53)

But even more importantly, these other sources help bring to life and reveal the absolute truth of our Savior and King, Jesus the Messiah. His life, death and future coming was foretold and prophesied over four hundred times in the Old Testament before the birth of Christ. Jesus made it very clear that the Old Testament spoke of him and prophesied about him when he stated:

"You diligently study the Scriptures because you think that by them you possess eternal life. These are the Scriptures that testify about me." (John 5:39)

You would think that eventually, after two thousand years of research, everything has already been written, everything investigated, and eventually the case closed on the case for Christ in finding all the truth, the clues and the eventual verdict to the claims that he is the Messiah, the Son of the living God. But that is not the case. It just continues. And this is what makes the Bible so unique and so much fun when you choose to go deep into the words, thoughts, prophesies, and theology of the most influential man who has ever walked the earth. The treasures of truth, love, and forgiveness are never-ending in the pursuit of authenticity when it comes to the Scriptures, the Good News of Jesus Christ.

"And remember, our Lord's patience gives people time to be saved. This is what our beloved brother Paul also wrote to you with the wisdom God gave him—speaking of these things in all of his letters. Some of his comments are hard to understand, and those who are ignorant and unstable have twisted his letters to mean something quite different, just as they do with other parts of Scripture. And this will result in their destruction." (2 Peter 3:15–16)

I would like to touch on one more subject regarding the early church, the Gospels, the Scriptures, and how they correlated in actual time. This information might just surprise you. In the amazing and award-winning series *The Case for Christ*, we find one more amazing fact that I never knew before until I read it in *Lee Strobel's* books. Let me first set you up with some of the dialogue that *Lee* is discussing with *Craig L. Blomberg, PhD,* author of *The Historical Reliability of the Gospels.*

The discussion they are having is wrapped up in investigating how some scholars try to debunk Jesus's divinity by suggesting that the Resurrection was merely a mythological idea that developed over long periods of time. And also, that the Gospels were written so far after the actual events that legend corrupted the eyewitness accounts of Christ's life, therefore turning Jesus from merely a wise teacher into the supposed Son of God. Let's jump in and listen to their dialogue as they dismantle this secular view.

Introduction: Dialogue from his book, *The Case for Christ*, in chapter 1, *The Eyewitness Evidence*, with *Lee* stating some ideas about ancient writings:

"It's one thing to say that the gospels are rooted in direct or indirect eyewitness testimony; it's another to claim that this information was reliably preserved until it was finally written down years later." (p. 32)

"'To me, it seemed intuitively obvious that the shorter the gap between an event and when it was recorded in writing, the less likely those writings would fall victim to legend or faulty memories." (p. 33)

"'Let's get back to the dating of the gospels,' Lee said. 'You indicated that you believe they were written sooner than the dates you mentioned.'

"'Yes, sooner,' he said. 'And we can support that by looking at the book of Acts, which was written by Luke. Acts ends apparently unfinished—Paul is a central figure of the book, and he's under house arrest in Rome. With that the book abruptly halts. What happens to Paul? We don't find out from Acts, probably because the book was written before Paul was put to death.'

"Blomberg was getting more wound up as he went. 'That means Acts cannot be dated any later than A.D. 62. Having established that, we can then move backward from there. Since Acts is the second of a two-part work, we know the first part—the gospel of Luke—must have been written earlier than that. And since Luke incorporates parts of the gospel of Mark, that means Mark is even earlier.

"'If you allow maybe a year for each of those, you end up with Mark written no later than about A.D. 60, maybe even the late '50s. If Jesus was put to death in A.D. 30 or 33, we're talking about a maximum gap of thirty years or so.'

"He sat back in his chair with an air of triumph. 'Historically speaking, especially compared with Alexander the Great,' he said, 'that's like a news flash!' (The two earliest biographies of Alexander the Great were written by Arrian and Plutarch more than four hundred years after Alexander's death in 323 B.C., yet historians consider them to be generally trustworthy.)

"Indeed, that was impressive, closing the gap between the events of Jesus' life and the writing of the gospels to the point where it was negligible by historical standards. However, I still wanted to push the issue. My goal was to turn the clock back as far as I could to get to the very earliest information about Jesus.

GOING BACK TO THE BEGINNING

"I stood and strolled over to the bookcase. 'Let's see if we can go back even further,' I said, turning toward Blomberg. 'How early can we date the fundamental beliefs in Jesus' atonement, his resurrection, and his unique association with God?'

"'It's important to remember that the books of the New Testament are not in chronological order,' he began. 'The gospels were written after almost all the letters of Paul, whose writing ministry probably began in the late '40s A.D. Most of his major letters appeared during the '50s. To find the earliest information, one goes to Paul's epistles and then asks, 'Are there signs that even earlier sources were used in writing them?'

"'And,' I prompted, 'What do we find?'

"'We find that Paul incorporated some creeds, concessions of faith, or hymns from the earliest Christian church. These go way back to the dawning of the church soon after the Resurrection.

"'The most famous creeds include Philippians 2:6–11, which talks about Jesus being "in very nature God," and Colossians 1:15–20, which describes him as being "the image of the invisible God," who created all things and through him all things are reconciled with God "by making peace through his blood, shed on the cross."'

"'Those are certainly significant in explaining what the earliest Christians were convinced about Jesus. But perhaps the most important creed in terms of the historical Jesus is 1 Corinthians 15, where Paul uses

technical language to indicate he was passing along this oral tradition in relatively fixed form.'

"Blomberg located the passage in his Bible and read it to me:

"For what I received I passed on to you as of first importance: that Christ died for our sins according to the Scriptures, that he was buried, that he was raised on the third day according to the Scriptures, and that he appeared to Peter, and then to the Twelve. After that, he appeared to more than five hundred of the brothers at the same time, most of whom are still living, though some have fallen asleep. Then he appeared to James, and then to all the apostles." (Paul, 1 Corinthians 15:3-7)

"And here's the point,' Blomberg said. 'If the Crucifixion was as early as A.D. 30, Paul's conversion was about 32. Immediately Paul was ushered into Damascus, where he met with a Christian named Ananias and some other disciples. His first meeting with the apostles in Jerusalem would have been about A.D. 35. At some point along there, Paul was given this creed, which had already been formulated and was being used in the early church.

"'Now, here you have the key facts about Jesus' death for our sins, plus a detailed list of those to whom he appeared in resurrected form—all dating back to within two to five years of the events themselves!

"'That's not later mythology from forty or more years down the road. A good case can be made for saying that Christian belief in the Resurrection, though not yet written down, can be dated to within two years of that very event.

"'This is enormously significant,' he said, his voice rising a bit in emphasis. "'Now you're not comparing thirty to sixty years with the five hundred years that's generally acceptable for other data—you're talking about two!'

"I couldn't deny the importance of that evidence. It certainly seemed to take the wind out of the charge that the Resurrection—which is cited by Christians as the crowning confirmation of Jesus' divinity—was merely a mythological concept that developed over the long periods of time as legends corrupted the eyewitness accounts of Christ's life. For me, this struck especially close to home—as a skeptic, that was one of my biggest objections to Christianity." (Lee Strobel, *The Case for Christ*, p. 33–36)

With all the information that we currently have and have continued to study, uncover, verify, and confirm, it leaves no doubt in my mind that what I choose to believe in is rock solid.

Only in **his** hands do we experience the love, grace and pure mercy of our Lord and Savior, Jesus Christ. To **him**, I give ALL the glory. Thank you, Jesus…I love you.

"You will seek me and find me when you seek me with all of your heart." (Jeremiah 29:13)

"The Son of God became a man to enable men to become the sons of God." (C. S. Lewis)

"The more you read the Bible, the more you will fall in love with the author." (Anonymous)

"All Scripture is inspired by God and is useful to teach us what is true and to make us realize what is wrong in our lives. It corrects us when we are wrong and teaches us to do what is right. God uses it to prepare and equip his people to do every good work." (Paul, 2 Timothy 3:16–17)

Chapter 3

Thief

"These people honor me with their lips, but their hearts are far from me. Their worship is a farce, for they teach man-made ideas as commands from God."

—Isaiah 29:13

"'Jesus called a little child to him and put him among them. Then he said, 'I tell you the truth, unless you turn from your sins and become like little children, you will never get into the Kingdom of Heaven. So anyone who becomes as humble as this little child is the greatest in the Kingdom of Heaven. And anyone who welcomes a little child like this on my behalf, is welcoming me.'"
—Jesus, Matthew 18:2–5

"Someone once asked Billy Graham, 'If Christianity is valid, why is there so much evil in the world?' To which he replied, 'With so much soap, why are there so many dirty people in the world? Christianity, like soap, must be personally applied if it is to make a difference in our lives.'"

Throughout our lives, there are so many times when we feel unworthy and unloved. Some more than others. I am sure that most people would admit that life has been challenging, lonely, and painful. A struggle to find reasons to take another step, or to even get out of bed and to not give in to the temptation of ending their pain once and for all.

There is a song that is very dear to my wife's heart that helped her get through a very difficult time of her life. She was struggling to find hope, purpose, and the truth that Jesus loved her truthfully and unconditionally. My wife, Lena, had been on a journey to find what all of us have been looking for…love and acceptance…a relationship. But as many of us tend to do, we end up looking in all the wrong places. Or as Buckwheat (portrayed by Eddie Murphy) from the Little Rascals has famously sang it, *"Wookin' panub in all da wong paces…wookin' panuuuub!"*

She had accepted Christ years earlier, but much like my own journey, she had not yet developed her *relationship* with Christ. Sadly, she had just found out that the man she was in a relationship with was cheating on her and her life seemed to be going nowhere fast, spiraling out of control.

Lena was struggling to find purpose, to find a reason and a meaning for her life. Like many of us, if not all of us, at one moment in our life, she contemplated suicide, but instead chose to sit in her room crying uncontrollably and just listen to a song from one of her new favorite Christian bands, *Third Day*, over and over again. That song literally saved her life.

That song is titled "*Thief*" and is based on the Gospel of Luke 23:33–43. Here are the lyrics to the song which, coincidentally, is also one of *my* favorites.

> *I am a thief. I am a murderer…walking on this lonely hill.*
> *What have I done? No, I don't remember, no one knows just how I feel.*
> *And I know…that my time…is coming soon.*
> *It's been so long, oh such a long time. Since I've lived with peace and rest.*
> *Now I am here, my destination, I guess things work for the best.*
> *And I know…that my time…is coming soon.*
> *Who is this man? This man beside me yah, they call the King of the Jews?*
> *Well, they don't believe him, that he's the Messiah, somehow…I know that it's true.*
> *They laugh at him in mockery and they beat him 'till he bleeds, and they nailed him to the rugged cross and they raised him, yah, they raised him up next to me, yah.*
> *My time has come and I am slowly fading, but I deserve what I receive.*
> *Jesus, when you, enter your kingdom, could you please, please remember me, yah*
> *Well, he looks at me still holding on, and the tears fall from his eyes and he says I tell the truth,*
> *You, you will be with me in paradise*
> *Oh yah, and I know that my time is coming soon, I know my time is coming soon*
> *And I know, that paradise is coming soon…is coming soon.*
> (Third Day, "Thief")

In the Gospel of Luke, Jesus has just been put on trial before Pontius Pilate. Pilate finds him innocent but the leading priests and religious leaders, the Sanhedrin, along with most of the people, demand that he be put to death. Pilate offers to have him flogged and then to just release him, but to no avail.

"Then a mighty roar rose from the crowd, and with one voice they shouted, 'Kill him, and release Barabbas to us!' (Barabbas was in prison for taking part in an insurrection in Jerusalem against the government, and for murder). Pilate argued with them, because he wanted to release Jesus. But they kept shouting, 'Crucify him! Crucify him!'" (Luke 23:18–21)

So eventually Pilate sentenced Jesus to die by crucifixion, as they demanded. In Luke chapter 23, verses 32–43 it says,

"Two others, both criminals, were led out to be executed with him. When they came to a place called The Skull, they nailed him to the cross. And the criminals were also crucified— one on his right and one on his left.

"Jesus said, 'Father, forgive them, for they don't know what they are doing.'

"And the soldiers gambled for his clothes by throwing dice.

"The crowd watched and the leaders scoffed. 'He saved others,' they said, 'let him save himself if he is really God's Messiah, the Chosen One.' The soldiers mocked him, too, by offering him a drink of sour wine. They called out to him, 'If you are the King of the Jews, save yourself!' A sign was fastened above him with these words: 'This is the King of the Jews.'

"One of the criminals hanging beside him scoffed, 'So you're the Messiah are you? Prove it by saving yourself—and us, too, while you're at it!'

"But the other criminal protested, 'Don't you fear God even when you have been sentenced to die? We deserve to die for our crimes, but this man hasn't done anything wrong.' Then he said, 'Jesus, remember me when you come into your Kingdom.'

"And Jesus replied, 'I assure you, today you will be with me in paradise.'"

This story, like so many others that are wrapped up in this man Jesus, are incredibly powerful and life changing. We struggle to understand such mercy and forgiveness even while he is being tortured, mocked and murdered in the most despicable way possible.

"Father, forgive them, for they don't know what they are doing." (Jesus, Luke 23:24)

So much pain and loneliness, abandoned and all alone, he suffered and died for one single purpose...and that purpose was *us*. Through agonizing pain and mind numbing torture he chose us and in so doing, took our place on the cross with the complete weight of the world's sin on his shoulders. Can there be any greater example of love than this?

This truth tugs at the heartstrings of our very souls. We try and contemplate such an act of this magnitude filled with love and forgiveness while suffering such intense pain that we cannot even fathom its possibility. And yet, even now, this seems almost impossible. How could someone, anyone, be choosing to offer forgiveness at a time of such agony, loneliness, and despair?

This truth is what has given my wife hope, as well as myself, throughout our lives. It gave us hope to believe that we were still worthy of his love no matter how deep the hole that we had dug for ourselves. Even while sitting at the bottom of our misery, deep in our shame, our crap and our sin, he was reaching down, again and again, calling out to us "take my hand, I still love you, I still believe in you and"...

"I have plans for you," declares the Lord," plans to prosper you and not to harm you, plans to give you hope and a future." (Jeremiah 29:11)

How many of you reading this book have been there? Or are possibly there right now? I can personally say that I have been there far too many times, going through my own hell on earth, and gratefully, I lived to tell about it. Because I, too, needed Jesus in my life to pull me out of some deep dark trenches that I had once again buried myself within.

This is just one of those examples.

Like everyone else who is on this journey, we all long for a "normal" life. I wanted a life that was fulfilled in my relationship with God. I wanted a relationship that was grounded in our faith and that was healthy and had purpose. I wanted to grow with someone that loved God as much as I did.

But sadly, I allowed my temptations to rule my world instead of relying on God. Again and again, I found myself wrapped up in a relationship that was toxic and unhealthy.

In my twenties, I met a woman who fulfilled that temptation and desire. I struggled in every direction with this woman and paid a heavy price for my inability to walk away and just say no. Sadly, it became an addiction that would shackle me for years and no matter what I tried, I became stuck in this extremely toxic relationship. Eventually, she became pregnant and vehemently shouted with absolute certainty that this child was undeniably mine and no one else's. Deep down, though, I had a sickening suspicion that there was a good chance, however, that this baby had a different father.

With a soft heart and a caring disposition, I chose to care for this baby and give them a home knowing full well that she was most likely incapable of providing a proper environment to care for him.

Over the course of a few years, things began to crumble and our relationship was dissolving. Because of my poor choices and her dishonesty, we became bankrupt. With everything falling apart she decided it was in her best interests to leave me and in doing so, shackled me with the responsibility of paying child support for the next sixteen years. This became the catapult in choosing to find out once and for all if this child was truly mine or not.

I ventured into Seattle to get a proper DNA test done to clarify the truth. With little surprise, sure enough, this child was, in fact, not mine after all. This truth, I hope you know, was all at once bittersweet. I had developed a relationship with this child; I was this child's daddy. I was all he ever knew and now, here I was, in this dilemma of pure sadness, mixed with overwhelming relief knowing full well that I would not have to be financially strapped in my broken mess.

I thought thoroughly about what to do next. Do I try and stay in his life? Would that be the best course of action? He is only two years old, maybe he will forget who I am if I just walk away. If I don't walk away, will I ever be free of this woman who had tormented me for far too long? After what seemed like forever in the process of coming to a final decision, it seemed only obvious that unless I let go, I will be stuck in the chaos and insanity of this woman for a good portion of my life…and I did not want that.

Disheartened and filled with devastating guilt and grief over choosing to let him go, which was so extremely hard, I slowly had to rebuild my life once again. And once again, I felt I had "failed God" and myself. I didn't know where to turn and how to live "life" with all of my broken pieces.

The beautiful part of this painful and sad story is that God never left my side…not once. I had to come back to Him, crawling on my hands and knees, tears streaming down my face, humble and repentant. I knew that God wanted what was best for me; I knew *He* wanted to be the center of my life but I didn't believe I deserved it. I didn't feel or act like someone who deserved to be loved unconditionally with all of my poor choices, sexual addiction, selfishness, and my inability to be strong and say no to the temptations and sin.

But that is where I was dead wrong. You see, if your heart is genuinely longing for Christ and you truly *want* to be forgiven…if you have a repentant and remorseful heart…He hears you and He will forgive you even though he knows you will NEVER be sinless. God already knows this and He loves us anyway. That is *amazing grace…* that is *no-condemnation love* for those who are in Jesus Christ. But you have to be in Jesus and Jesus has to be in you.

If you are not a Christian but you want to know this freedom, all you need to do is ask Jesus into your heart. Pray to him. Repent of your sins and let go of your sinful past and let the healing power of Jesus begin to penetrate your heart so you can be free at last!

The Gospels are filled with truth and love. But are also filled with warnings and second chances.

"Don't you fear God even when you have been sentenced to die?" (Luke 23:40)

Quite honestly, we are all sentenced to die. You may think you have a long time here on this earth, but I am here to tell you, it is more like a blink of an eye. I am almost fifty. Those fifty years went by very, very fast. And I didn't eat so well most of those years, which worries me a bit. Too much ice cream, chocolate milk, and cinnamon rolls.

I am not scared to die, but I also want to live and experience what it is like to be a grandpa. I don't even have my first grandbaby yet! But I am certainly looking forward to that time when I get to snuggle with them, play with them, and then send them on home with their parents. I hear that it is truly a wonderful thing, being a grandparent.

Life has a way of teaching us many things even when we don't ask to learn them.

Throughout most of my childhood, my young life and into my early twenties, I was a thief. I usually tried to steal anything that was not nailed down. I remember as early as kindergarten, and this is going to sound as bad as it was, when the kids would bring in their show and tell items and display them in the room somewhere, if it was small enough, I stole it. The teacher would be pleading with all of us to please return the item that had been stolen, and I just had to have it. Honestly, I don't know what sparked this in me or why I felt that it was even okay to do such a thing, but I did it and I was pretty good about getting it done.

I would even go so far as to steal my neighbor's hot wheels. Then, I would take them to my house, bury them in the dirt, unbury them, and pretend that I just uncovered a treasure. That only worked once by the way and then my parents were on to me. If I remember correctly, we didn't have a lot of money. We wore second-hand clothes and usually bought most of our toys at Goodwill or some other second-hand store.

Finders keepers, losers weepers. This carried on into my teenage years, and if you read my first book, *This Thing Called Life*, then you know all about my adventures in stealing. Needless to say, it did eventually catch up to me and thank goodness for that, because not too long after I got caught, I finally came to my senses and stopped that silliness. But mainly it was because I finally grew up and was convicted by the Holy Spirit about the things that needed to change.

Those criminals that were hanging there alongside of Jesus for a moment in time were for a moment…Jesus's neighbors. And in that short six hours of time that Jesus was with them, hanging there nailed to the cross beam, he gave them hope, grace, love, and forgiveness. Unfortunately, as the story goes, only one of the two men chose to believe that this man, Jesus, was the Son of God.

Imagine for a moment that these two men, while in sheer agony of unspeakable torture, had a chance to communicate with Jesus, knowing full well that they were on their death bed, and only one of them chose to reach out to Jesus, asking him simply to remember him. Yes, he did rebuke the other criminal for his disbelief, but he did not deny his own sin. He knew that his choices had put him on that cross and that Jesus was innocent. And yet, the thief didn't ask Jesus to take him into paradise with him but to just remember him…"*Remember me.*" Jesus took it one step further and said, "*You will be with me in paradise.*"

Can you even imagine, how that man felt? Here he was, hopeless, frightened, tortured, and alone, dying a slow and painful death. Then, all of a sudden, he wasn't alone. Realizing that he had just been given a second chance, even while he was near death, he merely believed and then reached out to Jesus and asked if he would simply remember him. Wow! Powerful stuff.

"*Jesus forgave a thief dangling on a cross, knowing full well the thief had converted out of PLAIN FEAR. That thief would never study the Bible, never attend synagogue or church, and never make amends to those he had wronged. He simply said "Jesus remember me," and Jesus promised, "Today you will be with me in paradise." It was another shocking reminder that grace does not depend on what we have done for God but rather what God has done for us.*" (Philip Yancey, *The Jesus I Never Knew*)

I have often visualized, or tried to imagine, what that scene in all of its agony and pain would look like…feel like. I have seen many attempts of recreating the crucifixion scene through movies and plays. It must have been one of the most incredible, if not *the* most incredible scene to have witnessed.

Try to envision for a minute, all the dialogue that has been happening up to this final event. The mission work of Jesus, the healings, the sermons, the parables, the miracles, the life transformation of so many people, the feeding of the five thousand, and the raising of the dead. To have been a witness to all the controversy surrounding Jesus. All the time while following him and listening to him preach wisdom that seems to be coming from somewhere else than from this "ordinary Jew."

And yet, he surprised them with his knowledge, his wisdom of the Scriptures and many Jewish leaders, the Pharisees, tried to trick him into saying something that would give the Romans a reason to arrest him and kill him. Jesus spoke without fear, stood up to the Sanhedrin, the religious leaders of that time, and challenged them in every way from their faith to how they followed God. He challenged every Pharisee and Jew that listened to him preach to live a life the opposite of what they were living. Love those who persecute you, love, not hate. Give to those who take from you. Love your enemies even while the Romans were killing and ravaging their possessions, taxing them beyond what they can handle. All the while they were believing that a Messiah would come and save them.

I have to admit, loving your enemies has to be one of the most difficult choices we will ever choose to make in this life. I cringe when I read about a parent whose child was brutally murdered, and yet, this parent chooses to forgive them, and forgive them face-to-face willingly. I cringe because I know that if this becomes a part of my story then this is what I must choose to do also, but if I was to be put in that same scenario, would I follow through with it, could I actually do it?

"After saying all these things, Jesus looked up to heaven and said, 'Father, the hour has come. Glorify your Son so he can give glory back to you. For you have given him authority over everyone. He gives eternal life to each one you have given him. And this is the way to have eternal life—to know you, the only true God, and Jesus Christ, the one you sent to earth. I brought glory to you here on earth by completing the work you gave me to do. Now, Father, bring me into the glory we shared before the world began.'" (Jesus, John 17:1–5)

Jesus knew his time was coming to an end. His prayers to the Father were almost always with regard to the ones he was trying to save and to serve. His love for us was immeasurable and I just love hearing Jesus's plea to the Father for us. He is truly our advocate.

"Now I am coming to you, I told them many things while I was with them in this world so they would be filled with my joy. I have given them your word. And the world hates them because they do not belong to the world, just as I do not belong to the world. I am not asking you to take them out of the world, but to keep them safe from the evil one.

"They do not belong to this world any more than I do. Make them holy by your truth; teach them your word, which is truth. Just as you sent me into the world, I am sending them into the world. And I give myself as a holy sacrifice for them so they can be made holy by your truth.

"I am praying not only for these disciples but also for all who will ever believe in me through their message. I pray that they will all be one, just as you and I are one—as you are in me, Father, and I am in you. And may they be in us so that the world will believe you sent me." (Jesus, John 17:13–21)

With all the drama leading up to this one event, the crucifixion, it was almost as if all the Jews present, the leaders of religious law, the Romans, the apostles, the Pharisees, the guards, the scribes, the unbelievers, and the followers of Jesus were all standing there, waiting, watching him, hanging up there on that tree, helpless as a baby…that they all needed to see one more amazing, mind blowing miracle to prove his claim that he was truly the Son of God.

"By this time it was about noon, and darkness fell across the whole land until three o'clock. The light from the sun was gone. And suddenly the curtain in the sanctuary of the Temple was torn down the middle. Then Jesus shouted, 'Father, I entrust my spirit into your hands!' And with those words he breathed his last. When the Roman officer overseeing the execution saw what had happened, he worshipped God and said, 'Surely this man was innocent.' And when all the crowd that came to see the crucifixion saw what happened, they went home in deep sorrow." (Luke 23:44–48)

They wanted to see if he would somehow, miraculously, come down off that cross and *save himself.* But instead, they went home in *"deep sorrow,"* seeing the final result of another dead man, another prophet, hanging there, on a tree, dead to the cruelties and false accusations of his Jewish brothers, screaming for death while Pilate tried to negotiate life to no avail. Now they believed he was nothing more than a good man who preached some good sermons, performed all those miracles, but yet, he was not the Messiah they were looking for.

How ironic is it then, that over two thousand years later, we are still debating and contemplating if not only what has happened is true, but also, that his claim to be the Messiah, the Son of God, is also valid and true?

No doubt this man, Jesus, was a man that would never be forgotten. A man of such historical significance that he would be causing the division of mankind even now, two thousand years later. But let us not forget that this man came from a small part of a very big world yet unexplored and insignificant. How is it then, that a story of this magnitude and insignificance could have stood the test of time, how could this story have been told…and then told again? Written down and shared and shared again to eventually have reached the ears and souls of billions upon billions of people over the course of two thousand years?

People who have been touched so deeply by this story chose to even lay down their life out of love and faithfulness. Never refuting it, but living by its every word? If he was not so profound, so memorable and so majestic and awe-inspiring in his example of his life then why are his life and words still so prevalent and ground breaking even now, so many years later?

We cannot simply throw off this profound fact as simply being a historical phenomenon. He is STILL turning the world on its head and it is still spinning from the insurmountable evidence of the life-transforming love and sacrifice he showed us then and is still showing us now.

Three days later, after his brutal death on the cross, as predicted throughout the Gospels by Jesus and in the Old Testament, he did save himself. But that was not his mission. His mission was to save *US* and give us a reason for hope, for truth, for a way out from our misery, brokenness, loneliness and addictions.

Music has been a very important part of my life. It too, has brought me through some very trying and difficult times and through some of my most dark and painful experiences that I will never forget. Through my twenties and into my thirties, I listened to *Margaret Becker*. A female Christian artist that really gave me hope at a time when I didn't feel I deserved God's love because I had failed him so many times. This was before I truly knew what unconditional love meant. Before I knew what Romans 8:1–2 actually meant.

"So now there is *No Condemnation* for those who belong to Christ Jesus. And because you belong to him, the power of the life-giving Spirit has freed you from the power of sin that leads to death." (Paul, Romans 8:1–2, emphasis mine)

Sharing through her songs, *Margaret Becker* knew very well the overwhelming power of what guilt and shame can do to you as you feel hopeless to the sin that continues to ravage your soul. But her songs were deep and full of raw truth. She inspired my heart and gave me hope because of the loving redemption of Jesus Christ that she sang about within her lyrics and through the heaviness of her soulful voice. She helped me to realize and believe that he still loves me so very much despite my struggles and despite my lack of faith.

We try and we try again. Failure after failure, we begin to feel like there is no hope. "How could God even for one minute look down upon me and see any value...any worth? He must hate me... despise me. He must think that I am a hopeless loser. My own dad never thought much about me...why would our Father in heaven think any different?" These thoughts become prevalent and begin to sound like a broken record.

Or maybe this is what you are saying to yourself: "I have been told about this man, Jesus, who loves me so much to have done the unthinkable and die for me, for us. But yet, when I try so hard to be good, to be sinless and not give in to temptation I still fail…well then, why would I be deserving of such a gift as this? How could someone continue to love a loser like me? It is pretty obvious to me that I am certainly not meant to go to heaven, step foot in a holy church, or to be so lucky to be forgiven, when all I do is think about what I want and how badly I want to do what I am not supposed to do."

All these thoughts running through your head are a constant barrage of negative inputs, insults, and beliefs that you are not worthy, not valuable, surely not loved or wanted. These thoughts, when repeated over and over again, will eventually establish a message of complete failure, telling you that you cannot win against the sin and temptation of this world that is overwhelming you.

This was my battle cry for years. Struggling to understand the concept that no matter what, Jesus loved me. I was a thief, and he loved me. I was a sex addict, but he still loved me. I was a liar, and a failure, a thief…and I hurt people…but he still loved me…how can this be? It doesn't make any sense…*How?!* Simply put…grace and mercy.

"So then, since we have a great High Priest who has entered heaven, Jesus the Son of God, let us hold firmly to what we believe. This High Priest of ours understands our weaknesses, for he faced all of the same testing we do, yet he did not sin. So let us come boldly to the throne of our gracious God. There we will receive his mercy, and we will find grace to help us when we need it most." (Hebrews 4:14–16)

"We are made right with God by placing our faith in Jesus Christ. And this is true for everyone who believes, no matter who we are.

"For everyone has sinned; we all fall short of God's glorious standard. Yet God, with undeserved kindness, declares that we are righteous. He did this through Christ Jesus when he freed us from the penalty for our sins. For God presented Jesus as the sacrifice for sin." (Paul, Romans 3:22–25)

"Therefore, since we have been made right in God's sight by faith, we have peace with God because of what Jesus Christ our Lord has done for us. Because of our faith, Christ has brought us into this place of undeserved privilege where we now stand, and we confidently and joyfully look forward to sharing God's glory.

"We can rejoice, too, when we run into problems and trials, for we know that they help us develop endurance. And endurance develops strength of character, and character strengthens our confident hope of salvation. And this hope will not lead to disappointment. For we know how dearly God loves us, because he has given us the Holy Spirit to fill our hearts with his love." (Paul, Romans 5:1–5)

"So now we can rejoice in our wonderful new relationship with God because our Lord Jesus Christ has made us friends of God." (Paul, Romans 5:11)

In this next passage of scripture, the Apostle Paul is explaining his own struggles in dealing with his own sin, making it evident that no one is free from the challenges of temptation because of the sinful nature that is present in all of us. All of us struggle with the sinful nature at war within us. Praise be to God for his insurmountable love in sending his Son as a sacrifice for our sins so we could ultimately be set free from sin and death, free from guilt and shame…and free to love ourselves again so we, in turn, can love others with the love of Jesus Christ.

"So the trouble is not with the law (the Ten Commandments) for it is spiritual and good. The trouble is with me, for I am all too human, a slave to sin. I don't really understand myself, for I want to do what is right, but I don't do it. Instead, I do what I hate. But if I know that what I am doing is wrong, this shows that I agree that the law is good. So I am not the one doing wrong; it is sin living in me that does it.

"And I know that nothing good lives in me, that is, in my sinful nature. I want to do what is right, but I can't. I want to do what is good, but I don't. I don't want to do what is wrong, but I do it anyway. But if I do what I don't want to do, I am not really the one doing wrong; it is sin living in me that does it.

"I have discovered this principle of life—that when I want to do what is right, I inevitably do what is wrong. I love God's laws with all my heart. But there is another power within me that is at war with my mind. This power makes me a slave to sin that is still within me. Oh, what a miserable person I am! Who will free me from this life that is dominated by sin and death? Thank God! The answer is in Jesus Christ our Lord.

"So you see how it is: In my mind I really want to obey God's law, but because of my sinful nature I am a slave to sin." (Paul, Romans 7:14–25, emphasis mine)

In the very next chapter he starts with the verse that gave me hope at a time when I felt completely hopeless and helpless. In my own evaluation of myself and my sin, I came to believe the lie that this is also how God saw me through his eyes. But this verse, which I mentioned earlier in this chapter, literally changed my life and my perception that even with all of my faults, all of my sins, Jesus truly did love me and would never leave me. And that even with my inability to be sinless, I was loved and cherished, adored, and a child of God.

I did not lose my salvation because of my struggles with sin… but because of his amazing grace…I was redeemed and continuously restored in his kindness and acceptance of me. I repented of my sin and this truth would be the catapult to propel me into a whole new existence of my life and the desire to be more like Jesus every day. And quite honestly, I have never been the same since.

"So now there is no condemnation for those who belong to Christ Jesus." (Paul, Romans 8:1)

There have been no sweeter words ever said to me. And with that truth, I am forever grateful. I am no longer condemned for my sins, I am redeemed. I am no longer a slave to the temptations of sin; I am free from the guilt and shame of my past, present, and future.

Life and all that it has to offer is where our challenge begins. We almost instantly, once we are old enough to understand, have to sort and sift through the garbage and the gunk...to get to the heart and meat of what is truly relevant and of great worth. It seems as though, for us to get to the sincere and solid truth of unconditional love, we have to go about it the hard way. We have to fall, fail, and make mistakes. We are hurt by people and then we hurt people. Hopefully, along the way, we find the truth we are looking for. Real truth, not the lies the world wants to tell you, but the truth that changes the world. The truth of pure love, pure joy, pure wisdom, and pure forgiveness.

We are all searching for this truth. It is up to each and every one of us to sort out what is the most valuable amongst all that is present. Our time here is short, our days clicking down...don't miss the chance to follow your heart and uncover the truth of what God has planned for you. I can only pray that the light I am attempting to shine will shine bright enough to open your eyes to the reality of the world and the beautiful truth of our Lord and Savior, Jesus Christ.

Even now, today, I still struggle to believe that I am doing all that I can in my relationship with Jesus. Every day I have to seek his grace and remember that he loves me even if I don't feel worthy. Yes, I am writing a book about Jesus, my relationship with him and all that...but I struggle to believe that it is enough. Each of us has to mentally, spiritually and emotionally choose to love and believe in a God that is unseen. We choose to believe in God by faith.

"For we live by believing and not by seeing." (Paul, 2 Corinthians 5:7)

And yes, there are doubts, but what happens in the process of this relationship with him is the undoubtable love, unconditional love that comes pouring in through our soul, through our life and through the belief that all hope is not lost in this myriad of craziness that is life on a planet so full of despair, hatred, war, violence, selfishness, and the murdering of innocent babies. The struggle is no longer about...if I should live...but *how* can I live *to please God?*

We tend to grow up believing we need to please people. Please our parents, please our children, our teachers, our coaches and bosses. Please our siblings and our peers, our best friends. Then we experience disappointment, abandonment and many forms of abuse, lack of fairness, favorites, distrust, cheating, lying and infidelity. Pain shows its ugly and distorted face time and time again until we become unsure of what relationships really look like…or can they be trusted?

Then Jesus steps in and grace says, "I love you just the way you are and will always love you no matter what."

We venture into life a brand-new human being, a baby, just like Jesus did. Jesus experienced life, dirty diapers, hunger, temptation, pain, struggle, abuse, abandonment, sadness, loneliness…just like the rest of us. He understands what we are going through and his grace is enough.

When we can come to that understanding is the moment when we realize that *THE* most important relationship is not with your parents, your children, your spouse or significant other…it is with Jesus. Every other relationship will then be exposed by its unhealthiness or just the opposite, by its beautiful blessing, deserving of our time and investment. The toxicity of a bad and unhealthy relationship should be terminated so that you can then invest your time, your energy and your heart into the relationships that are blossoming as a result of your relationship with Jesus.

Please understand that God loves everyone. Even the ones that are sick and evil, but that does not mean you have to put up with the sick and evil of that person in a relationship. Step away, as far away as you can so you can become healthy and find healing and growth within your relationship with Christ. Pray for them and if it is possible, forgive them, but also ask for forgiveness and make amends with them. You must also forgive the ones who hurt you. This is not an easy choice to make. But I guarantee you…it is the most freeing choice you will ever make.

The suggestions I am making here are a direct reflection from my own experiences and choices that I had to make in my own life and certainly may not have the same challenges or even the same level of results you are looking for. I am just telling you what I had to do and the hard choices I had to make so that life could have a chance to drastically change for the better. It is never easy to say goodbye… but it might be the best goodbye you could ever make, and, it is in *your* best interest to do so.

Once you have become healthy, then you can find the relationships that will continue to help you grow and prosper in the most important relationship…and that is with Christ.

This takes a lot of time. Years of understanding, growth, maturity, healing of your past, these are all necessary steps to the process of a healthy relationship. Jesus wants a relationship with you. He wants to care for you and take upon his shoulders the burdens you once carried. Relationship…not religion.

Please understand, though, this is life, and life will continue to be hard and challenging even in your relationships when you put Jesus first. There will be times when you feel like your world is crashing all around you, and that you can't quite understand what you did to receive all this carnage. Just remember, this is not retaliation from God because of something you did (or didn't do). It is just life and sometimes life deals us all a bad hand. Just stay strong, stay the course and put your faith in Jesus. He will be your rock in unsettling situations. And through all that transformation the results will be understanding and wisdom to guide your relationships helping you to see which connections bring you closer to him and which ones need to be severed. Putting our hope, our trust, and our faith in him is the first step.

You, like one of the two thieves hanging next to Jesus, have a choice. You can either mock him and be left to die alone in your misery, selfishness, and sin, or you can reach out to God and ask him to remember you. Ask him to forgive you and ask him into your heart and your life. Ask him for help with your sin, your addictions, your challenges, and your pain. This is the beginning of an amazing and beautiful relationship. Life is truly never the same. It is never easy, but with the hope and faith that you can have with Jesus, you can love again.

I have learned what it means to forgive. I have come to the complete realization that there is nothing more valuable on earth than knowing and loving Jesus Christ and being in a relationship with him. Not religion but a relationship. Uncover this truth and never stop searching…for one day we will be with him in paradise.

Today could be the first day of the rest of your life. And with Jesus by your side, as your neighbor, as your friend and as the lover of your soul…you will never be alone again.

"Can anything ever separate us from Christ's love? Does it mean he no longer loves us if we have trouble or calamity, or are persecuted, or hungry, or destitute, or in danger, or threatened with death? (As the scriptures say, "For your sake we are killed every day; we are being slaughtered like sheep.) No, despite all these things, overwhelming victory is ours through Christ, who loved us. (Paul, Romans 8:35–37)

"You see, we don't go around preaching about ourselves. We preach that Jesus Christ is Lord, and we ourselves are your servants for Jesus's sake. For God, who said, 'Let there be light in the darkness,' has made this light shine in our hearts so we could know the glory of God that is seen in the face of Jesus Christ.

"We now have this light shining in our hearts, but we ourselves are like fragile clay jars containing this great treasure. This makes it clear that our great power is from God, not from ourselves.

"We are pressed on every side by troubles, but we are not crushed. We are perplexed, but not driven to despair. We are hunted down, but never abandoned by God. We get knocked down, but we are not destroyed. Through suffering, our bodies continue to share in the death of Jesus so that the life of Jesus may also be seen in our bodies." (Paul, 2 Corinthians 4:5–10)

Chapter 4

We Are Known by Our Fruit

"Teach those who are rich in this world not to be proud and not to trust in their money, which is so unreliable. Their trust should be in God, who richly gives us all we need for our enjoyment. Tell them to use their money to do good. They should be rich in good works and generous to those in need, always being ready to share with others. By doing this they will be storing up their treasure as a good foundation for the future so that they may experience true life."

—Paul, 1 Timothy 6:17–19

"For whatever is in your heart determines what you say. A good person produces good things from the treasury of a good heart, and an evil person produces evil things from the treasury of an evil heart. And I tell you this, you must give an account on judgment day for every idle word you speak. The words you say will either acquit you or condemn you."
—Jesus, Matthew 12:34–37

"If you are in a position to help someone, help them. God just might be answering that person's prayer through you."

—TobyMac #speaklife

Observance and perception.

What our eyes see and what fills our thoughts as we perceive the world around us is driven by these two actions. We are constantly observing all that is around us and listening to hopefully find some truth. As we filter through our levels of wisdom, intelligence, and our experiences, we are hoping to find what we have already chosen to believe despite our ignorances. Then we choose to judge as to what is right and what is wrong according to what we think we know as fact, or even more so, based on our level of faith, or the lack thereof, in what we are hearing or perceiving.

The world around us is a never-ending spinning top with thousands of vibrant colors, thoughts, words and actions being thrown at us in a continual experience of life. We take in all the information, chew on it and then spit out what we don't want to accept as fact, truth or faith. What we keep inside though, what we swallow and digest, is then categorized into thousands of different folders, each with its own name attached to it.

Daily and almost regularly, we are sifting through these files that we have chosen to accept as truth to then either apply them to our lives or save them for when they will be needed to teach, communicate or debate our beliefs. Or when the time is right, you will choose a file to bring up again at a later date to do more research, ask more questions, watch and observe to see if what is actually being said could and will come to fruition. And finally, after some debate or with some added truth or findings that help cement your beliefs, there are files that will be deleted. But how deep do we truly go to find that truth?

By simple standards, the complexity of our world and everything that it consists of, is by far, a vast and endless array of the most creative, bizarre and mind blowing effects of nature, the elements, light and dark, and the air we breathe, space and time continuum, down to the sheer complexity of the human anatomy.

For example, the human eye is divinely complex and most of us take our vision for granted. The ability to see thousands of different colors in the various canvases of the gorgeous landscapes that cover this planet is simply breathtaking. Just recently, we have been able to create a pair of glasses that gives to those who are either color blind or who don't see colors at all, the opportunity to wear them and see what they have been missing out on their whole lives. Their reactions are priceless. They begin to cry uncontrollably at the simple array of rainbow colors they are experiencing for the very first time. What they are seeing literally takes their breath away and they are mesmerized by the glorious creation all around them leaving them extremely emotional to the vastness of the beauty they have been missing all along.

Let me take a minute to explain the complexity of the human eye. The retina, for example, conducts close to *ten billion* calculations every second, and that is before an image even travels through the optic nerve to the visual cortex. In a normal eye, the light rays come to a sharp focusing point on the retina. The retina functions like the film in a camera...the retina receives the image that the cornea focuses through the eye's internal lens and transforms this image into electrical impulses that are carried by the optic nerve to the brain. Wait just a tick. What? Whoa! Okay, I don't know about you but that is flipping fascinating and mind-blowing all at the same time. And yet, we pass over this like it is nothing out of the ordinary. How does that happen and why?

Here is something else to think about for a minute. There are literally thousands of processes that are taking place all the time just as complex as the functioning of the human eye. In fact, there are trillions of chemical reactions taking place in every one of your cells every second. Allow me to repeat that last statement…trillions… every cell…every second. Your body is almost continuously digesting food, inhaling oxygen, exhaling carbon dioxide, repairing tissues, maintaining equilibrium, producing hormones, purifying toxins, metabolizing energy and circulating blood every minute and at every moment you are awake and/or sleeping. And as you read this, millions of electrical impulses are firing across billions of synaptic pathways in your brain without even thinking about it. Umm…hello… this should be blowing your mind, metaphorically speaking!

How is it that something so complex can be easily passed over as ordinary? When do we get to that point in our lives when all the miracles that take place right in front of us become almost pointless and either do not compute as miraculous or are pushed aside like an empty plate after its food has been consumed? How can the world and all of its millions upon millions of functioning parts be discarded as simply ordinary? How do most of us overlook this reality every day and never stop to think how it all came into being?

I was thinking the other day how incredible wind is. Think about it for a moment. Where the heck does wind come from? How can it be that the wind just came about from nothing? In a moment we are walking along minding our own business and then out of nowhere and completely unseen, we are swept up with our hair blowing every which way, with leaves fluttering and dancing in mid-air, our clothes being shifted and thrown about…but yet…we don't give it one thought…but instead, we curse at it for messing up our beautiful hair-dos. But yet, there it is. Wind. Invisible but also apparent in the matter it touches. We can only see it when it is moving an object like a leaf, a tree or a branch. We can certainly hear it as it swims past us at an alarming rate. It is there one minute…gone the next. Crazy.

Our lives are full of so much information that is being exposed to us at a very rapid rate and somehow we are able to shuffle through it, categorize it, file it, ignore it, or dismiss it.

As we perceive the world and all its inhabitants around us, we, as human beings, judge both the landscape around us and the actions and words of every individual we come in contact with. Believe it or not. It is an automatic repulsive action that we are not even aware we are doing, when, in fact, that is exactly what we are doing. Most of the behaviors and characteristics that we have attached to our persona are there because you have chosen to keep them there. You have picked them up along the way and they are a part of who you are, your life experiences and your story. Scars, war wounds, and all.

What we have chosen to become will be seen and heard through our actions, words, and lifestyle. What we have grown up to see and experience will have a direct relation to the actions of our life, our words and the way we choose to live life and treat others. It will also determine the path of your life, what you believe and what you choose to invest your time, energy, money, faith, and yes, even your own heart and soul into. The tragedies, the beauty of nature, the miracles and also the beautiful highlights of our lives eventually become emulated in the actions of our lives.

There were many, many different things my parents did that I knew right away I never wanted to be a part of who I was and how I would raise my own children. But the ugly head of truth and my experiences did eventually effect how I chose to react in my parenting. But here is the beautiful thing about all this: we can choose to change what it is we don't like and do not want in our lives, change what is in our own personality at any time or any day of our life.

I realized right away what I was doing within my negative reactions and also the unhealthy actions that were directly related to my upbringing. Then, I claimed it. I chose to cut it out of my life for the sake of my children's lives. I chose to change. I chose to make it an absolute necessity to give my children a better life that is void of the unhealthy and toxic behaviors, words, and actions of the destructive parenting I received.

We have the power to change; we have the ability to choose a different path. We just have to believe we can and then do it with determination, purpose and prayer.

We can choose to be different at any time throughout the sequence of our life's story.

And we can change the outcome of our story at any time or any day…you just have to believe that you can.

Quite simply, my strength comes from the choice of believing that I, alone, cannot do this thing called life on my own. I need to believe that there is something far greater outside myself. And only because of what I have seen with my own eyes, experienced with my own hands, and felt with my own heart and soul, do I believe that the hope that is within me is found in my relationship with my Savior and my creator, Jesus Christ.

We are all in an elevator going up and down, every day of our lives. We're randomly getting off at this floor and that floor looking to find something to help us make sense of what this life is all about. Pushing the buttons to the next floor. Floor 18, please. Searching, prying, digging and filtering all the information that is seeping through. Whatever we choose to attach to ourselves will be seen by everyone and judged by everyone. How do you want to be represented?

"This is your life, are you who you want to be?" (Switchfoot, *This Is Your Life*)

This quote that I found in a song really spoke to me, like many songs do, in such a way as to ask a really hard question about who I was and who I had chosen to be. *Are you who you want to be?*

Throughout the New Testament, the term, Good Fruit, is used many times to describe the true essence, the true dimensions, the character, behavior, attitude and finally the actions of a man or woman.

"You will know them by their fruit."

"Beware of false prophets, who come to you in sheep's clothing, but inwardly they are ravenous wolves. You will know them by their fruit, that is, by the way they act. Do men gather grapes from thorn bushes or figs from thistles? Even so, every good tree bears good fruit, but a bad tree bears bad fruit. A good tree cannot bear bad fruit, nor can a bad tree bear good fruit. Every tree that does not bear good fruit is cut down and thrown into the fire. Yes, just as you can identify a tree by its fruit, so you can identify people by their actions." (Jesus, Gospel of Matthew 7:15–20)

The world and the people around you will either produce a positive or a negative response depending on how you choose to act or react.

"The emotions we experience don't reflect external reality; they reflect internal reality. We don't see the world as it is; we see the world as we are. So wonder, or the lack thereof, simply reveals what is in our souls. If our souls are full of wonder, then life is wonderful. Why? Because you see with your soul. And when you see with your soul, everything becomes a reflection of God." (Mark Batterson, Primal)

We will either choose a dark path or we will choose a path that is full of light. We will either live with regret, shame, bitterness, jealousy, hatred, and anger or we will find a way to forgive, love again, see the blessings and find healing. But the results of your life choices will affect you and will eventually surface for all to see. Especially in your words and in your actions. They will know you by your fruit.

To be content in this world with what we have is a challenge and a temptation we all face on a daily basis. Especially for those of us who have been blessed enough to have been born in a first world country. The challenge is real and the retail marketing world knows this to the greatest extent. It is mind boggling to fathom what would happen to the world if people became content with what they have and decided that they no longer needed to "upgrade" anything. That we would no longer need to buy expensive cars, houses, clothes, phones, or any of the other things this world deems important. You will never see this, though…not in our lifetime.

"Yet true godliness with contentment is itself great wealth. After all, we brought nothing with us when we came into the world, and we can't take anything with us when we leave it. So if we have enough food and clothing, let us be content." (Paul, 1 Timothy 6:6–8)

"The purpose of my instruction is that all believers would be filled with love that comes from a pure heart, a clear conscience, and genuine faith. But some people have missed this whole point. They have turned away from these things and spend their time in meaningless discussions." (Paul, 1 Timothy 1:5–6)

For many who are searching, they are doing what they need to do. For I believe we are all a continuous work in progress that truly never ends. God is perfecting us through our faith and our good works. This is also a choice that must be a reflection of God's transformation of your heart and your life. The resulting gratitude should be in the attitude you display for all to see. The gift of salvation is the most precious gift you can ever be given. Until you understand and accept the magnitude of this *present* in your life you will struggle to understand or feel the *presence* of Christ in your life.

Our lives are destined for death and even death eternal if we choose a path of darkness and not the path of Jesus Christ. We have been warned time and time again of the consequences of our actions and of our choices if we so choose to denounce the free gift of God's salvation. There is no grey area in the truths and understanding of what Jesus is telling us throughout his Gospels and in every book of the Bible. Choose wisely, then, how you live your life!

"You can enter God's Kingdom only through the narrow gate. The highway to hell is broad and its gate is wide for the many who choose that way. But the gateway to life is very narrow and the road is difficult, and only a few ever find it." (Jesus, Gospel of Matthew 7:13–14)

"Not everyone who calls out to me 'Lord, Lord' will enter the Kingdom of Heaven. Only those who actually do the will of my Father in heaven will enter. On judgment day many will say to me, 'Lord, Lord! We prophesied in your name and cast out demons in your name and performed many miracles in your name.' But I will reply, I never knew you. Get away from me, you who breaks God's laws." (Jesus, Gospel of Matthew 7:21–23)

"Anyone who listens to my teaching and follows it is wise, like a person who builds a house on solid rock. Though the rain comes in torrents and the floodwaters rise and the winds beat against that house, it won't collapse because it is built on bedrock. But anyone who hears my teaching and doesn't obey it is foolish, like a person who built a house on sand. When the rains and floods come and the winds beat against that house, it will collapse with a mighty crash." (Jesus, Gospel of Matthew 7:24–27)

But for those who are searching to know who Jesus is and if he truly is the Son of God, please know this… He is always waiting for you with open arms to come to him because he loves you passionately. He came for the lost, the hurting, the sick and the despised. He came for the outcasts, the broken, the less than and for those who are without hope. He came for all of us, all walks of life, all nations and nationalities.

"As Jesus was walking along, he saw a man named Matthew sitting at his tax collector's booth. (Matthew was also a tax collector) 'Follow me and be my disciple,' Jesus said to him. So Matthew got up and followed him.

"Later, Matthew invited Jesus and his disciples to his home as dinner guests, along with many tax collectors and other disreputable sinners. But when the Pharisees saw this, they asked his disciples, 'Why does your teacher eat with such scum?'

"When Jesus heard this, he said, 'Healthy people don't need a doctor—sick people do,' Then he added, 'Now go and learn the meaning of this Scripture: "I want you to show mercy, not offer sacrifices." For I have come to call not those who think they are righteous, but those who know they are sinners." Jesus, Matthew 9:9–13, emphasis mine)

"If you cling to your life, you will lose it; but if you give up your life for me, you will find it." (Jesus, Matthew 10:39)

Our lives consist of the daily demands of work, careers, childrearing and marriage, all screaming our names and asking us to submit to them, day after day. We all look forward to the day of rest and hopefully some years of retirement in the future, believing that life will be pleasant and stress-free once that day arrives. But at what cost? My father worked his whole life to enjoy five measly years of retirement. Don't get me wrong, his last five years were like heaven on earth, but that was the extent of it. Five years and then his life was over. And sadly, he chose to live those last few years far away from all of his kids and grandkids. A choice that hurt me personally.

We spend most of our lives working to live in such a way as to have all the things we think we need. Of course we need the essentials like food, shelter, heat, clothing, clean water and clean air. But what else? Our way of life and all that we work for is a choice based around how much stuff we think we need.

Once upon a time…the mom stayed at home to take care of the kids and the house while the dad went to work to bring home the bacon to throw in the frying pan. Now, both parents work and the kids run the house throwing the bacon up against the wall.

Our choices define us and shine a bright light onto who and what we have chosen to become and they also reveal what we have deemed the most important part of what we believe ourselves to be. Our fruit clearly defines our character and our character defines our integrity. Our integrity defines our choices and actions which in turn reveals how much we choose to love or despise others in our lives, especially those who we love the most.

If we love God, then our lives should show it. If we love people, then our actions should reveal that in how we live our life. Are we living out our faith or are we disguising it with fulfilling the duties that we have come to believe will justify getting us into heaven? Do you feel you are justified because you go to church every Sunday? Or that you have a devotional that you are always reading? Are you putting it on the calendar to make sure you are reading the Bible all the way through each year on a daily basis?

These are all wonderful things we should be doing…but let me ask you this: Are you serving outside the church? Are you looking for opportunities to help the less fortunate? Do you sponsor children from around the world in third world countries? Are you faithful in your tithing? Do you look for opportunities to serve others knowing you will receive nothing in return? Are you being obedient to the call on your heart?

Are you truly living out your life with an example of the love and light of Jesus, every day and in every situation? Are you even close to acting, living and breathing a Christ-like life? Do people assume you are a "Christian" simply by watching and listening to how you live your life, what you say and how you treat others?

Jesus needs soldiers and warriors who are ready to move and answer the call to make a difference in this world. We are ALL warriors for Christ if we sincerely believe and call ourselves "Christians."

"So also Jesus suffered and died outside the city gates to make his people holy by means of his own blood. So let us go out to him, outside the camp, and bear the disgrace he bore. For this world is not our permanent home; we are looking forward to a home yet to come.

"Therefore, let us offer through Jesus a continual sacrifice of praise to God, proclaiming our allegiance to his name. And don't forget to do good and to share with those in need. These are the sacrifices that please God." (Hebrews 13:12–16)

Our mission field is not in a church building and it is not checking off a bunch of boxes to make sure you have fulfilled the title of being righteous. Please don't misunderstand me. There are many important jobs and positions that are required and are needed to be fulfilled through the body of Christ and each of us need to find our gift and where we can be instrumental to serving others. We have all been given a special gift or talent that is instrumental in meeting the needs of the church and the needs of the less fortunate.

What I am asking is this…have you ever ventured out into the Great Adventure that God wants to take you on? So that your fruit will be in abundance, pouring over and touching lives in a way you can never even imagine? So that others will see your abundance, your joy, your love and zest for life and will want to know "how do I get that?"

The abundance I am mentioning here is not money, or accolades, but the reward of doing God's work through us, the hands and feet of Christ. There are so many avenues we all can seek out and find to serve others, and to find ways to love others in such a way as to change their lives and greatly change yours along the way.

"If you are wise and understand God's ways, prove it by living an honorable life, doing good works with humility that comes from wisdom." (James 3:13)

"But the wisdom from above is first of all pure. It is also peace loving, gentle at all times, and willing to yield to others.

It is full of mercy and good deeds. It shows no favoritism and is always sincere. And those who are peacemakers will plant seeds of peace and reap a harvest of righteousness." (James 3:17-18)

"So humble yourselves before God. Resist the devil, and he will flee from you. Come close to God, and God will come close to you. Wash your hands, you sinners, purify your hearts, for your loyalty is divided between God and the world. Let there be tears for what you have done. Let there be sadness instead of laughter, and gloom instead of joy. Humble yourselves before the Lord, and he will lift you up in honor." (James 4:7-10)

God's word is truth. It is also humbling and full of grace.

God only wants to give you the best life possible...but not exactly the life you dreamed of. All of us have to be willing to see and understand that this life, our life, is...not...about...us. It is about Jesus. This life you have, that you think is yours...it's not yours... it's his. And when we come to that full understanding we will either embrace it with joy or we will act like the rich ruler who walked away saddened by the reality that he would have to give up his riches to be a follower of Christ.

"Someone came to Jesus with this question: 'Teacher, what good deed must I do to have eternal life?' 'Why ask me about what is good?' Jesus replied. 'There is only One who is good. But to answer your question—if you want to receive eternal life, keep the commandments.'

"'Which ones?' the man asked. And Jesus replied: 'You must not murder. You must not commit adultery. You must not steal. You must not testify falsely. Honor your father and mother. Love your neighbor as yourself.'

"'I've obeyed all these commandments,' the young man replied. 'What else must I do?' Jesus told him, 'If you want to be perfect, go and sell all your possessions and give the money to the poor, and you will have treasure in heaven. Then come, follow me.'

"But when the young man heard this, he went away sad, for he had many possessions. Then Jesus said to his disciples, 'I tell you the truth, it is very hard for a rich person to enter the Kingdom of Heaven. I'll say it again, it is easier for a camel to go through the eye of a needle than for a rich person to enter the Kingdom of God!'

"The disciples were astounded. 'Then who in the world can be saved?' they asked.

"Jesus looked at them intently and said, 'Humanly speaking, it is impossible. But with God all things are possible.' Then Peter said to him, 'We've given up everything to follow you. What will we get?'

"Jesus replied, 'I assure you that when the world is made new and the Son of Man sits upon his glorious throne, you who have been my followers will also sit on twelve thrones, judging the twelve tribes of Israel. And everyone who has given up houses or brothers or sisters or father or mother or children or property, for my sake, will receive a hundred times as much in return and will inherit eternal life. But many who are the greatest now will be least important then, and those who seem least important now will be the greatest then.'" (Jesus, Matthew 19:16–30, emphasis mine)

The truth hurts and our lives consist of choosing the right path…the path of a servant. Not so easily said as done. Again and again, Jesus points back to the heart of a man or woman and asks us: *"What will you choose?"* It is simply quite obvious and yet we try and skim right past the truth that is so evident in the words of the Gospels and the example that Jesus Christ left for us to see and admire. *Will you lower yourself to a servant, as I have done, will you choose to serve others and think of them before yourself?* Because if you choose to lose your life, for the sake of Jesus and his Kingdom, you will save it.

"Before the Passover celebration, Jesus knew that his hour had come to leave this world and return to his Father. He had loved his disciples during his ministry on earth, and now he loved them to the very end. It was time for supper, and the devil had already prompted Judas, son of Simon Iscariot, to betray

Jesus. Jesus knew that the Father had given him authority over everything and that he had come from God and would return to God. So he got up from the table, took off his robe, wrapped a towel around his waist, and poured water into a basin. Then he began to wash the disciples' feet, drying them with the towel he had around him.

"When Jesus came to Simon Peter, Peter said to him, 'Lord, are you going to wash my feet?'

"Jesus replied, 'You don't understand now what I am doing, but someday you will.'

"'No,' Peter protested, 'you will never ever wash my feet!'

"Jesus replied, 'Unless I wash you, you won't belong to me.'

"Simon Peter exclaimed, 'Then wash my hands and head as well, Lord, not just my feet!'

"Jesus replied, 'A person who has bathed all over does not need to wash, except for the feet, to be entirely clean. And you disciples are clean, but not all of you.' For Jesus knew who would betray him. That is what he meant when he said, 'Not all of you are clean.'

"After washing their feet, he put on his robe again and sat down and asked, 'Do you understand what I was doing? You call me "Teacher" and "Lord," and you are right, because that's what I am. And since I, your Lord and Teacher, have washed your feet, you ought to wash each other's feet. I have given you an example to follow. Do as I have done to you.'" (Jesus, Gospel of John 13:1–15)

Which is it then? Which will you choose?

Trust me when I tell you, that choosing to follow Christ is a life full of abundance and joy, laughter and tears, miracles and answers to prayer. There will be tears of incredible love and giving, unwavering mercy and unending grace. Your life will most surely never be the same. It certainly does not guarantee peace or safety from the world, for the world hates us and the message we are trying to tell and live out. Life has a way of challenging us, tempting us to go in the opposite direction. It comes down to a choice. The most important choice of your life.

We all have a purpose in this life and Christ wants to fulfill the purpose for which you were created. We just have to be willing and obedient to the call. But we first have to align our hearts, our minds and our lives in the direct pathway and light of Jesus. Until we do that…and choose to surrender our lives…it will be difficult, just as it was for the rich ruler to sell all of his possessions he held so dearly to the point of not being able to let go of them. Until then, we will fight to keep what we believe is ours. We will control it, consume it, and hang on to it for dear life believing in its security instead of trusting in God.

Our fruit is shown in our ability to be humble and obedient to our Lord and Savior, Jesus Christ. It is he who is calling us to a higher standard. But he is also calling us to a much more fulfilling life full of good fruit.

"The greatest among you must be a servant. But those who exalt themselves will be humbled and those who humble themselves will be exalted." (Jesus, Gospel of Matthew 23:11–12)

Personally, I believe one of the most amazing and mind-blowing things about choosing to sincerely follow Christ is seeing him work through you to drastically change the life of another. To physically see the dimensions of your giving, your love and your service to those who have less, or just need love and support, is a feeling of pure joy, pure soul moving, tears-a-flowing, life changing and heart transforming experience after experience and it will revamp your life like nothing else on earth. Trust me when I tell you this.

"We need leaders not in love with money but in love with justice. Not in love with publicity but in love with humanity." (Martin Luther King Jr.)

The treasures you are storing in heaven are the treasures your soul is experiencing right here on earth. Don't miss out on a life that is filled with adventure, excitement and a story you never thought possible as it unfolds just as Jesus had already planned once you came to believe and trust in him.

The life you choose to lead in Christ will be a life either admired from a distance or it will move others so deeply they will experience the joy they see in your life and will naturally gravitate toward the light that shines from you and through you.

"What good is it, dear brothers and sisters, if you say you have faith but don't show it by your actions? Can that kind of faith save anyone? Suppose you see a brother or sister in need, who has no food or clothing, and you say, 'Good-bye and have a good day; stay warm and eat well'—but then you don't give that person any food or clothing. What good does that do?

"So you see, faith by itself isn't enough. Unless it produces good deeds, it is dead and useless." (James 2:14–17)

The story of *Ebenezer Scrooge* and the *Grinch* both tell a similar story of the transformation of the heart when we truly see with our eyes and are touched with our hearts to move into action and change the world around us by the love that grows in our souls. The branches of the trees we bear should be healthy and heavy by the fruit we share. Be the one who chooses to change the world with every act of kindness by finding the opportunities to give to those who are in desperate need of our love and generosity.

Let your fruit be seen by all as a gesture of your love for the one that first loved you through the greatest gift ever given in his sacrifice on the cross. The first tree to bear fruit was the tree Jesus was nailed to, for us, so we can be free to love and forgive, have mercy on others and give generously and genuinely. Love the less fortunate, be kind to everyone, and give to those who so desperately need us in Jesus's name.

"So be truly glad. There is wonderful joy ahead, even though you have to endure many trials for a little while. These trials will show that your faith is genuine. It is being tested as fire tests and purifies gold—though your faith is far more precious than mere gold. So when your faith remains strong through many trials, it will bring you much praise and glory and honor on the day when Jesus Christ is revealed to the whole world.

"You love him even though you have never seen him. Though you do not see him now, you trust him; and you rejoice with a glorious, inexpressible joy. The reward for trusting him will be the salvation of your souls." (1 Peter 1:6–9)

I seriously love God's word. It is ripe with good fruit, full of wisdom, overflowing with love and completely covered in the grace, forgiveness and mercy of Jesus Christ. Come to the light and never walk in darkness again.

"But the Holy Spirit produces this kind of fruit in our lives: love, joy, peace, patience, kindness, goodness, faithfulness, gentleness, and self-control. There is no law against these things!

"Those who belong to Christ Jesus have nailed the passions and desires of their sinful nature to his cross and crucified them there. Since we are living by the Spirit, let us follow the Spirit's leading in every part of our lives." (Galatians 5:22–25)

Chapter 5

Take Up Your Cross

"The message of the cross is foolish to those who are headed for destruction! But we who are being saved know it is the very power of God."

—Paul, 1 Corinthians 1:18

"His disciples came and asked him, 'Why do you use parables when you talk to the people?' He replied, 'You are permitted to understand the secrets of the Kingdom of heaven, but others are not. To those who listen to my teaching, more understanding will be given, and they will have an abundance of knowledge. But for those who are not listening, even what little understanding they have will be taken away from them.'"
—Jesus, Gospel of Matthew 13:12

I love science fiction, movies, and everything in between. To have been eight years old and sitting in a theater watching *Star Wars* when it first came to the big screen in 1977 was a sight to behold. It was an absolute thrill to experience such a monumental event in cinematic history. The following year for Christmas, I got an *X-Wing Fighter* with a *Luke Skywalker* action figure and a twelve-inch *Chewbacca* with a bandolier and a crossbow. So cool! (He was really a twelve-inch plastic doll but it sure was exciting.)

I love the fact that our minds have been designed with such a capacity that we can escape through our imagination at any time. We daydream almost instantaneously as we are driving to our distant destinations, often getting lost in our mind and soon forgetting where we were going.

But through our amazing, creative and beautiful minds, we have the opportunity to come up with some of the most marvelous and extraordinary stories that take us away from the reality of life's challenges. Can you imagine our world without *Star Wars*, *The Lord of the Rings*, *The Narnia Chronicles*, or *Winnie the Pooh*? Life (and even more so as a child), would be so much more dull and boring without the chance to be taken away to another world where we get to know characters like *C3-PO*, *Superman*, *Guardians of the Galaxy*, and *Gandalf the Grey*.

My movie library consists of hundreds of titles and many different genres ranging from the *Marvel* universe to romantic movies to even a few good ghost stories. I love dramas like *The Green Mile*, *Shawshank Redemption*, and *The Color Purple*, movies that consist of an awe-inspiring subject matter that reach deep into your soul and touch the deepest nerves that lie there. The human heart and your very soul need to be fed with the truth and love of the experience of life, and the goodness that is real and everywhere. Ask yourself these questions…

"Why is it that we love to see good triumph over evil? What is it that is so intriguing to us that we long for it, almost demand it?" Why are comic books and movies about super heroes and villains so popular? Why is it that we love to see real life stories of good conquering evil in our present day? Personally, I believe evil has been thoroughly present throughout the centuries and is still alive and well in the world around us and throughout the world we live in.

We are all constantly looking and hoping to see a shift in the balance of good vs. evil. We want to believe that truth will win over the lies and deception that seems so prevalent in our world. We are even going so far as to look for a savior in the silhouette of our president to hopefully change the dynamics of our society so we can feel better about our lives, our country, and our choices.

Throughout our world and throughout the existence of time, we have been working diligently to survive and to continuously find ways to save this planet that sustains life for all living things that we call earth. As far as we know, this is the only living planet with life, food, oxygenated air and a sustainable climate.

We, as the human race, are in a continuous battle fighting against the forces of evil every day within every single life. We grapple daily against mental sanity, the overconsumption of food, addictions, disease, abortion, and even in the greed of our own government. In less-fortunate countries, they are fighting against famine, slavery, terrorism, the massacre of different religions and struggling to find clean water that is not tainted with disease killing people at an alarming rate. Most of the world's population is living with less than they actually need to survive. And so it continues.

Every day we fight against crime, child trafficking, child pornography, homelessness and prostitution. We fight to save our marriages from abuse, pornography, drug and alcohol addiction and infidelity. We fight against the diseases of this world in AIDS and HIV, cancer and heart disease. We fight to keep drunk drivers off the roads and to maintain safe roadways to decrease highway casualties. The list of endless challenges is redundant and quite evident surfacing every day before our very eyes. But are we winning the battle?

I believe the answer to that question will only be answered when we begin to fully understand that we must first lose the battle to win the war.

The reason we long to see good triumph and seek to watch movies with only good and happy endings is because we WANT so badly to believe that good DOES win in the end. We want and we need to believe that through all of our tears, our sadness, our scars and disappointment, hard work, hopelessness, sacrifice, and eventually death...that there will be life and it will be life eternal.

I also believe this is why the story of Jesus Christ is one of the most profound, heartfelt and deep-rooted faiths in all of human history. How important is it then to seek out the truth and find it? When do we come to that true understanding that this life is the beginning of our eventual death? Without faith in an eternal God, does evil win over good because life ends in death? Only if we choose to believe it and therefore allow it. But I truly believe you must choose life first and that life is Jesus Christ.

"So we keep on praying for you, asking our God to enable you to live a life worthy of his call. May he give you the power to accomplish all the good things your faith prompts you to do. Then the name of our Lord Jesus will be honored because of the way you live, and you will be honored along with him. This is all made possible because of the grace of our God and Lord, Jesus Christ." (Paul, 2 Thessalonians 1:11–12)

The reason for the season of Christmas is based solely around the story of good conquering evil in the most popular of stories that is still being played out. Every day there is a huge celebration of so many people recovering from the addictions that they have conquered through AA and Celebrate Recovery. These programs give them tools to conquer their demons and past mistakes from a variety of addictions that consumed them, controlled them, and almost (if not already), destroyed their lives.

Through those programs and in the belief of a higher power, God, they have had the opportunity for a second chance at life. They learn how powerful forgiveness is in changing their lives and giving them hope once again. They learn how to make amends with those they have hurt, asking for forgiveness, which starts the healing process and are renewed once again in the loving arms and truth of Jesus Christ and each other. They find a safe place to unpack all their crap, be honest for once in who they were and are, while opening up all of their past sins and brokenness. They can finally take off their masks and be loved for who they are right here, right now—no matter what!

Those that have participated in these programs have found unconditional love, forgiveness, support and acceptance from the other members of the group. They stand for each other and encourage each other. They are there for each other in this struggle of life, finding worth in themselves again, rebuilding their lives and learning that we are all human and all of us are prone to making mistakes. We begin the process of learning how to do life differently and then we are able to forgive ourselves and find true love in the forgiveness and grace of our loving Savior, Jesus Christ.

Each and every one of us wants to believe that the story of Jesus is true, authentic and real. That this Jesus is truly our conquering hero who has promised to come back for us a second time to free us from the pain, sickness, and tyranny of the world we currently live in.

We long to put our hope into something to give us peace of mind and to wipe away our tears once and for all. In my opinion, there is no greater faith than in the belief of Jesus, our Savior and returning King.

"I urge you, first of all, to pray for all people. Ask God to help them, intercede on their behalf, and give thanks for them. Pray this way for kings and all who are in authority so that we can live peaceful and quiet lives marked by godliness and dignity. This is good and pleases God our Savior, who wants everyone to be saved and to understand the truth. For there is only one God and one Mediator who can reconcile God and humanity—the man Christ Jesus. He gave his life to purchase freedom for everyone." (Paul, 1 Timothy 2:1–6)

Over one hundred million Bibles are printed every year. One hundred million! Consumers in the United States alone will purchase 25 percent of those newly printed Bibles and in the world today there are more than 2,100 languages that have been translated and are available throughout the world of God's Good News. (Source: Brandon Gaille.)

These statistics are wonderful and all…but how often are they being read and studied? On average, the Christian household has seven to nine Bibles in their home. The question that dares to be asked is…are they collecting dust or are they changing lives? Are they being wielded like a sword in battle or have they become book ends? And if you are reading your Bible, do you feel like you are growing in your relationship with Jesus?

My one profound goal when I stand before Christ one day is to hear him say to me,

"Well done, good and faithful servant!" (Jesus, Matthew 25:23)

For those of us who have chosen to call ourselves Christians and who have a strong understanding of being a follower know full well that it means a lot more than just going to church and picking up your Bible every once in a while. It means diving in head first and getting deep into the words of Christ.

Once we are able to grasp the reality of our salvation through Christ, we grow, we learn, we cry, we embrace the truth of His mercy upon our lives. We start to absorb the full meaning of what it looks like in choosing to be a follower of Jesus.

Our lives are slowly transformed, our hearts softened, forgiveness is given and the purpose and deep meaning of the cross becomes crystal clear. We are on a journey of becoming like Christ and that means eventually picking up our own cross and choosing to follow his example.

"I have been crucified with Christ. It is no longer I who live, but Christ who lives in me. And the life I now live in the flesh I live by faith in the Son of God, who loved me and gave himself for me." (Paul, Galatians 2:20)

Twice in the Gospel of Matthew, Jesus calls on us to pick up our cross and follow him. First in Matthew 10:38–39,

"If you refuse to take up your cross and follow me, you are not worthy of being mine. If you cling to your life, you will lose it, but if you give up your life for me, you will find it."

Then again in Matthew 16:24–27. But first, let me give you some dialogue of what is taking place that leads up to this second warning from Jesus, to take up our own cross.

"From then on Jesus began to tell his disciples plainly that it was necessary for him to go to Jerusalem, and that he would suffer many terrible things at the hands of the elders, the leading priests, and the teachers of religious law. He would be killed, but on the third day he would be raised from the dead.

"But Peter took him aside and began to reprimand him for saying such things. 'Heaven forbid, Lord,' he said. 'This will never happen to you!'"

"Jesus turned to Peter and said, 'Get away from me, Satan! You are a dangerous trap to me. You are seeing things merely from a human point of view, not from God's.'

"Then Jesus said to his disciples, 'If any of you wants to be my follower you must turn from your selfish ways, take up your cross, and follow me. If you try to hang onto your life, you will lose it. But if you give up your life for my sake, you will save it. And what do you benefit if you gain the whole world but lose your own soul? Is there anything worth more than your soul? For the Son of Man [Jesus] will come with his angels in the glory of his Father and will judge all people according to their deeds." (Matthew 16:21–27, emphasis mine)

Let me clarify something here that I think is important to all that are seeking to know Jesus. When he is saying to his disciples…

"If any of you wants to be my follower…"

He is referring to all of us, not just his disciples. Okay then, what exactly does it mean to pick up your cross and follow him? In my personal opinion, it means that Jesus has to become the cornerstone of your life. He has to become the foundation to which all things revolve around. We must surrender to his will for our lives and realize that we are not in control, he is. It also means that we are to live out our lives choosing to be "Christ-like" or a true follower of Christ, suffering and all.

To me, it means your life is no longer yours. Let go of all you held so dear and begin the process of understanding what it means to be like Jesus. It is a transformation of the heart. You begin to see the world through the eyes and heart of Christ. And because you are choosing to go this way, you will have to suffer through that transformation.

Choosing to be a follower of Christ means you will have to eventually take up your own cross and suffer through the consequences of choosing HIS way instead of the ways of the world which only bring destruction, pain, selfishness, and greed. And trust me, this will be painful because you are choosing to go against the grain of all the temptations the world wants to offer you. You will have to fight against wanting to please people instead of pleasing God and sometimes, that hurts.

"For God called you to do good even if it means suffering, just as Christ suffered for you. He is your example, and you must follow in his steps. He never sinned, nor ever deceived anyone. He did not retaliate when he was insulted, nor threaten revenge when he suffered. He left his case in the hands of God, who always judges fairly. He personally carried our sins in his body on the cross so that we can be dead to sin and live for what is right. By his wounds you are healed. Once you were like sheep who wandered away. But now you have turned to your Shepherd, the Guardian of your souls." (1 Peter 2:21–25)

Trust me when I say this…it will bring you unfathomable joy in the understanding of what it means to lose your life for the sake of Christ. There is no greater sacrifice that you can make than to take up your cross and follow him…and no greater reward.

Jesus never sugar-coated anything with regard to what it looks like if you choose to truly follow him. You cannot be a lukewarm Christian who chooses only to follow Jesus when it is beneficial to you. Nowhere in the Bible is there a verse where it says you can just park your cross somewhere and come back and get it when it is beneficial to you and choose only what you want to do or only what you choose to believe. This is the fine line you must walk carefully, so as to not fall into the temptation of a prosperity Gospel or choose to become a pew warmer. Jesus makes it very clear.

Choose wisely then to understand what Jesus is asking us to do. Very bluntly and very plainly, Jesus is asking us to lay down our lives for the sake of the call.

After Jesus's resurrection from the dead and right before his ascension to heaven he asks Peter three times.

"Simon, son of John, do you love me more than these?" 'Yes, Lord,' Peter replied, 'you know I love you.' 'Then feed my lambs.' Jesus told him.

"Jesus repeated the question: 'Simon, son of John, do you love me?'

"'Yes, Lord,' Peter said, 'you know I love you.' 'Then take care of my sheep,' Jesus said. [Referring to his church and his followers]

"A third time he asked him, 'Simon, son of John, do you love me?' Peter was hurt that Jesus asked the question a third time. He said, 'Lord, you know everything. You know that I love you.'

"Jesus said, 'Then feed my sheep.'" (John 21:15–17, emphasis mine)

As human beings, we are prone to sin, temptation, weakness, poor judgment and poor choices. We simply have to proclaim our weakness as such and fall to our knees in worship and in prayer to the mercy and forgiveness of Jesus who loves us so very much. He is simply asking us, as he did Peter, "Do you love me, enough, to lay down your life for me?"

"Will you let me be in control of your life?"

"Will you trust me?"

It is an honor to be called by Jesus to follow him and be accepted into his family. I cannot imagine a life without him.

I have read several powerful and moving biographies of the lives of people being put in the utmost desecrating situations bordering on the brink of death and with unimaginable torture during WWII such as *Viktor Frankl* and *Corrie Ten Boom*. Even in the most desperate of times when there seems no hope, they found hope in Jesus. And sometimes hope is the only thing that keeps us going and keeps us striving to live a better life.

This is where the battle of good vs. evil truly takes place. In the hearts of men and women everywhere. We all have a choice to make every day. How will I choose to live out my life? What kind of person do I long to be? Do I desire to do good or evil? Am I giving back to the world a negative outcome because I feel it is warranted and I am entitled? Will I choose to pick up my own cross and follow him?

"I preached first to those in Damascus, then in Jerusalem and throughout all Judea, and also to the Gentiles, that all must repent of their sins and turn to God—and prove they have changed by the good things they do." (Paul, Acts 26:20)

We have a tendency to justify everything we do. We feel entitled as Americans that we deserve to own this or purchase that, to say this and do that. And if someone tries to stop us, well then, we will find a way to take it and enforce our will onto their lives. The corruption and greed is out of control even within our own government...but don't get me started on that.

Having seen firsthand the effects of a third-world country in parts of Uganda, Kenya and Mexico, it is an enlightening moment to understand personally and to see with my own eyes the depths of what Jesus truly means to those who are completely relying on him in faith to provide their most basic needs of life-sustaining food and clean water. Let us never forget that our most precious need that has to be met is our belief that we are loved and cherished. That we are important and that this life has purpose. This is where the most powerful and purest love in the world comes from. Our Lord and Savior, Jesus Christ.

When we have been stripped of all that matters to us with regard to personal belongings, loved ones, protection and comforts...trust me...if you haven't before, you will be crying out to God to save you from your torment, suffering and pain. Just ask the Jews, the gypsies, the gay and lesbian folks who were tortured and killed viciously from the Nazis of that era. Or ask the thousands daily around the globe who are being bullied, tortured, killed, and martyred for their beliefs in Jesus and in God.

In the luxuries of our "First World" problems, most of us have no idea what it means to suffer. We have not a clue as to what it means to live without, to be in fear of our lives and the lives of our families or to be in a place of utter reliance on God. The question we need to ask ourselves is… "Have I ever given my life over to Christ in such a way as to believe he is all I need and nothing more?" Or "Do I understand the depths of what it means to truly follow him?" Have you ever picked up your cross (to acknowledge and repent of all of your sins) and purposefully lost your life so that you can find it…in Him?

In the Gospel of John chapter 20, starting with verse 19, this is what it says:

"That Sunday evening the disciples were meeting behind locked doors because they were afraid of the Jewish leaders. Suddenly, Jesus was standing there among them! 'Peace be with you,' he said. As he spoke, he showed them the wounds in his hands and his side. They were filled with joy when they saw the Lord! Again he said, 'Peace be with you. As the Father has sent me, so I am sending you.' Then he breathed on them and said, 'Receive the Holy Spirit. If you forgive anyone's sins, they are forgiven. If you do not forgive them, they are not forgiven.'

"One of the twelve disciples, Thomas, was not with the others when Jesus came. They told him, 'We have seen the Lord!' But he replied, 'I won't believe it unless I see the nail wounds in his hands, put my fingers into them, and place my hand into the wound in his side.'

"Eight days later the disciples were together again, and this time Thomas was with them. The doors were locked; but suddenly, as before, Jesus was standing among them. 'Peace be with you,' he said. Then he said to Thomas, 'Put your finger here, and look at my hands. Put your hand into the wound in my side. Don't be faithless any longer. Believe!'

"'My Lord and my God!' Thomas exclaimed.

"Then Jesus told him, 'You believe because you have seen me. Blessed are those who believe without seeing me.'" (John 20:19-29)

"Faith is the confidence that what we hope for will actually happen; it gives us assurance about things we cannot see." (Hebrews 11:1)

The battle of good vs. evil was won that day when the Father lifted his Son, Jesus, from the depths of death and the empty tomb. What Christ had prophesied to his disciples in the Gospel of Matthew came true when he was arose from the dead. That momentous event was the turning point in all of human history shifting the balance of evil over to the victorious side of good. Of course this does not mean that evil is no longer present. But what it does mean is that we have hope. We have unconditional love and we no longer have to fear death.

The end of this story will not be one of sadness, fear, disappointment or experiencing the triumphant call of evil winning the war. The battle is in your heart and in your mind. We first must lose the battle of wanting to control our lives, being stubborn to believe we can do a better job at keeping evil at bay. We must first sacrifice our lives for the sake of Jesus so we can win the war of our souls and the souls of others.

It is useless and futile to believe we can do this life on our own. That we don't need a Savior to save us or that we have the capacity, intelligence or strength to combat the sin, temptation and evil of this world on our own. To win, you must first lose. And when you do… you will gain a life beyond anything you can imagine…and that is just what you will see and experience here on earth. Just think about what God has planned for us after this life is done!

"So then, since Christ suffered physical pain, you must arm yourselves with the same attitude he had, and be ready to suffer, too. For if you have suffered physically for Christ, you have finished with sin. You won't spend the rest of your lives chasing your own desires, but you will be anxious to do the will of God." (1 Peter 4:1-2)

I don't know about you…but I can't wait to see him and embrace the one who was sold out for me and took my place on the cross of shame, the cross of guilt and the cross of my overwhelming sin. To him, Jesus, do I owe my life and my love…and to him will I bow down and worship. For him, would I gladly pick up my own cross and carry it through suffering and pain, love, forgiveness and joy so that I may know him deeply and wonderfully. Carrying your own cross will change you. It will magnify the beauty and magnificence of what the symbol of the cross bears. Carrying your own cross will leave its mark and bring you closer to being like Christ. Good has already triumphed in this man, Jesus, the Son of the living God. The Good News is being shouted from the mountain tops! He is risen…
HE IS RISEN INDEED!

"I tell you the truth, you will weep and mourn over what is going to happen to me, but the world will rejoice. You will grieve, but your grief will suddenly turn to wonderful joy!" (Jesus, Gospel of John 16:20)

"Christianity has always insisted that the cross we bear precedes the crown we wear. To be a Christian one must take up his cross, with all its difficulties and agonizing and tension-packed content, and carry it until that very cross leaves its mark upon us and redeems us to that more excellent way which comes only through suffering." (Martin Luther King Jr.)

"For we don't live for ourselves or die for ourselves. If we live, it's to honor the Lord. And if we die, it's to honor the Lord. So whether we live or die, we belong to the Lord." (Paul, Romans 14:7-8)

"And so, dear brothers and sisters, I plead with you to give your bodies to God because of all he has done for you. Let them be a living and holy sacrifice—the kind he will find acceptable. This is truly the way to worship him. Don't copy the behavior and customs of this world, but let God transform you into a new person by changing the way you think. Then you will learn to know God's will for you, which is good and pleasing and perfect." (Paul, Romans 12:1-2)

Chapter 6

Mysterious Plan

"Devote yourselves to prayer with an alert mind and a thankful heart. Pray for us too, that God will give us many opportunities to speak about his mysterious plan concerning Christ. That is why I am here in chains. Pray that I will proclaim this message as clearly as I should. Live wisely among those who are not believers, and make the most of every opportunity."

—Paul, Colossians 4:2–5

"But don't be afraid of those who threaten you. For the time is coming when everything that is covered will be revealed, and all that is secret will be made known to all. What I tell you now in the darkness, shout abroad when daybreak comes. What I whisper in your ear, shout from the house-tops for all to hear!"
—Jesus, Matthew 10:26–27

"Those who leave everything in God's hands will eventually see God's hands in everything."
—Anonymous

Life.

In all its glory, what is it consumed of? What kind of price do we put on life? How valuable is it? What is truly important and how do we find true happiness? We each wake up, drink coffee (maybe?) and step through life day by day, not thinking twice about how much our lives are consuming.

How many of you are aware that our hearts are pumping two thousand gallons of blood each day to the arteries and veins throughout our bodies? Two thousand gallons! Or that the Earth is traveling close to one thousand miles per hour as we work, play, sleep, and watch TV?

Life and all that it has to show us is still one giant green and blue ball full of mysteries with new discoveries and subtle parts being revealed each day and year after year. Even after our so-called human intelligence has answered some of the mysteries surrounding us, and with all that our history has taught us, we are still befuddled by many more unanswered questions that are wrapped up in our lives, our bodies and throughout creation.

We think we have come to an understanding or have even come up with a hypothesis that would or should help explain as to the "what" and "why" we are here. It is an enigma that baffles us all when we finally reach that certain age of life as children where these questions just don't seem to have any answers.

So…we accept what is and move forward to make the best of it. Along the way, we learn and then learn some more. Listening to all the wisdom of our past and whatever makes its way into our minds, our hearts and our souls along the way. We watch the world unfolding before our very eyes and we are both delighted by it and depressed about it in the same moment.

We, as human beings, achieve wonderful new discoveries of species in plants, insects, and animals, but in the meantime continue to destroy the habitats that they are trying to survive in. We create new things to make our lives easier but in the process that very thing we created destroys life and brings more turmoil and pollution than we could have ever imagined. (Insert anything plastic here.)

We get excited about positive changes such as the Berlin wall being taken down or to see that we have been successful in bringing an animal species back off the endangered list. Then we turn right around and find out the greatest killer of humans last year was abortion at over 40 million worldwide…in one year…40 million babies! Let that sink in.

We spend billions of dollars on our pets each year but fail to see the value in human life. And this is because we believe we have the power to choose to make it that way. Broken, destructive, and greedy is the human heart without the presence of Jesus in our lives. No morals. Without the belief in a consequence of eternal death…we choose to live an ungodly life. It's my way or the highway. No guts, no glory. Is this really as good as it gets?

I don't know about you…but I want to go deeper. I want to hike further into the unknown and ask the even harder questions so that just maybe I could get a glimpse into something that is hidden just behind the curtain. To find more truth or to find a treasure that has been buried in a field. To locate an ancient artifact that will give me one more ounce of wisdom to understand the mysteries of what this life that we have been given is all about.

I want to be an Indiana Jones of God's word and discover the secrets and mysteries that lie hidden there, between the lines, but yet, are in plain sight.

Interesting side note here: It is quite ironic that two out of the three movies about *Indiana Jones* (I don't count the last one, that movie was horrible) are based around searching and finding biblical artifacts. The first being the Ark of the Covenant that encased the broken tablets of the Ten Commandments and Aaron's staff while the second artifact was the Holy Grail, which would be the chalice that Jesus drank wine out of at the Last Supper.

Anyway…back to the subject title of this chapter…

My youngest son, Ephram, loves the *Twilight Zone*. Just like when I was a kid, he loves watching how the show reveals stories of our crazy and puzzled world as it unfolds through the minds of the people who created those short stories. Each day is kind of like being in the *Twilight Zone* and searching for answers in the *Outer Limits*. We never know what the day's events will turn out like or where life will lead us to next.

None of us knows for sure if this present day here on earth will be our last or if we will live to be a hundred years old. Fear eventually becomes a part of our natural and regular everyday occurrence. Like an unwelcome next door neighbor who is constantly nagging us, emerging into our hearts and thoughts as we struggle to understand the process of life and the death that will eventually follow it.

Our fear is often found and is usually based around the questions that go unanswered surrounding tragedy, loss of life, disease, religious killings, war, natural disasters, and famine that seems to envelope our world. Why do these things happen and does God have any control over them?

Most of us just keep on moving forward believing that the only one we can truly trust in is…ourselves. We do everything we can and take every measure, every precaution to ensure the safety and protection of our children…and rightly so. Child trafficking is now a danger that none of us take lightly.

Most of the world's problems are grounded in the very sin we have allowed to consume us and overpower us, control us to the point of extreme unhealthiness, despair, and an eventual breakdown of the society we live in. Pornography, and especially child pornography, has warped the minds of too many men and is devouring the insatiable desires to the extent of kidnapping children to do unspeakable things to them. What has this world come to?

Greed is at least, if not the most, powerful drug and the most destructive force on the face of the planet. Greed is the consuming power which controls most of the sin that is rampant throughout our very diseased and extremely broken world. Behind the corruption of government, the empire of pornography, the chains of child trafficking, the death of drug addiction and the bloody wars lie the sour, rotting flesh, and deadly smell of greed.

Through every congress, every government, and every leader that is in charge and in power…greed lurks behind its ugly mask. Let us not be fooled by its false reality and its most revealing characteristic…the ultimate sin which leads to death. The fear is growing and the panic of the world is spreading. The question is being asked more and more, "Is there any hope for us in this world?" And even better yet, "Are we living in the end times?"

"Now the Holy Spirit tells us clearly that in the last times some will turn away from the true faith; they will follow deceptive spirits and teachings that come from demons. These people are hypocrites and liars, and their consciences are dead." (Paul, 1 Timothy 4:1–2)

We may not have all the answers to this *Rubik's Cube* of life and all that it is consumed by, but we have many avenues to venture into. Seek out their true nature and find the one answer that solves at least some of the mysteries that just might give us a light to follow, a choice to make, that will hopefully change the destiny of our lives from this destructive world and its evil lord of lies, greed, sin and tyranny to a life filled with love, unselfishness and forgiveness. A life that chooses to live for Christ.

"Here on earth you will have many trials and sorrows. But take heart, because I have overcome the world." (Jesus, John 16:33)

God's Word…the Good News…is packed full of never-ending wisdom and truth. But even more so it is filled to the brim with His love and forgiveness, life over death…His story. Just like I was mentioning in the last chapter, we are all looking, watching, and waiting to see how the universe unfolds. And who will win, the light side or the dark? Is there truly an unseen war taking place for our very souls that is happening between the forces of good and evil? According to what the Bible says (and I believe in it whole heartedly) the answer is yes.

"A final word: Be strong in the Lord and in his mighty power. Put on all of God's armor so that you will be able to stand firm against all strategies of the devil. For we are not fighting against flesh-and-blood enemies, but against evil rulers and authorities of the unseen world, against mighty powers in this dark world, and against evil spirits in the heavenly places.

"Therefore, put on every piece of God's armor so you will be able to resist the enemy in the time of evil. Then, after the battle you will still be standing firm." (Paul, Ephesians 6:10–13)

I believe that we are in a battle for our very souls and I also believe that each of us has an individual role in how this story will all play out. It is like the world is one expansive stage and we are each an actor or actress with our part in the play. Our lives, our choices, our words, and our actions…each time they are made either for the light or for the dark, sway the balance of how the Grand Finale of life and all of God's mysteries will eventually be unveiled. But when will this battle finally come to an end and will there be justice?

None of us know when this will end, not even Jesus.

"Later, Jesus sat on the Mount of Olives. His disciples came to him privately and said, 'Tell us, when will all of this happen? What sign will signal your return and the end of the world?' Jesus told them, 'Don't let anyone mislead you, for many will come in my name, claiming "I am the Messiah." They will deceive many. And you will hear of wars and rumors of wars, but don't panic. Yes, these things must take place, but the end won't follow immediately. Nation will go to war against nation, and kingdom against kingdom. There will be famines and earthquakes in many parts of the world. But all this is only the first of the birth pains, with more to come.

"'Then you will be arrested, persecuted, and killed. You will be hated all over the world because you are my followers. And many will turn away from me and betray and hate each other. And many false prophets will appear and will deceive many people. Sin will be rampant everywhere and the love of many will grow cold. But the one who endures to the end will be saved. And the Good News about the Kingdom will be preached throughout the whole world, so that all nations will hear it; and then the end will come.

"'Then if anyone tells you, "Look, here is the Messiah," or "There he is," don't believe it. For false messiahs and false prophets will rise up and perform great signs and wonders so as to deceive, if possible, even God's chosen ones. See, I have warned you about this ahead of time.

"'For as the lightning flashes in the east and shines to the west, so it will be when the Son of Man comes. Just as the gathering of vultures shows there is a carcass nearby, so these signs indicate that the end is near.

"'Immediately after the anguish of those days,

"'The sun will be darkened, the moon will give no light, the stars will fall from the sky, and the powers in the heavens will be shaken."

"'And then at last, the sign that the Son of Man [Jesus] is coming will appear in the heavens, and there will be deep mourning among all the peoples of the earth. And they will see the Son of Man coming on the clouds of heaven with power and great glory. And he will send out his angels with the mighty blast of a trumpet, and they will gather his chosen ones from all over the world—from the farthest ends of the earth and heaven.

"'However, no one knows the day or hour when these things will happen, not even the angels in heaven or the Son himself. Only the Father knows.

"'When the Son of Man returns it will be like the days of Noah. In those days before the flood, the people were enjoying banquets and parties and weddings right up to the time Noah entered his boat. People didn't realize what was going to happen until the flood came and swept them all away. That is the way it will be when the Son of Man comes.'" (Jesus, Matthew 24:3–14, 23–39, emphasis mine)

Jesus made sure that there were no doubts about his second coming, going so far as to give great details to the events as they would unfold before his return to save his chosen people. I believe I have found, throughout my studies over many years, some of the truths, hints and secrets that can help us understand some of the mysteries that Paul speaks of in many of his letters of the New Testament.

Nothing excites me more than when I discover a truth lying in plain sight buried within the Scriptures that opens another door to the dimensions of God's truths that he wants us to find. I believe it brings great joy to the Father when we uncover the mysteries that are right in front of us that lead to truth and a greater understanding of our purpose here in the grand scheme of this life he has given us.

First, let me take a moment to explain what it is I am stating here so as to not bring about a misunderstanding.

I am *not* proclaiming that I have found something that someone else hasn't already found. I am also not suggesting that I have found all the answers to the mysteries or secrets of God. That would be a foolish thing to say! What I am trying to explain is that I believe that God wants to show each of us something special that will relate to us individually for the purpose that he created us for. I believe he wants to pull back the curtain just a hinge to reveal something to each of us that brings about great joy, wisdom, hope, love, and understanding. If we seek him out…he will reveal the truth of the kingdom to us.

"I pray that from his glorious, unlimited resources he will empower you with inner strength through his Spirit. Then Christ will make his home in your hearts as you trust in him. Your roots will grow down into God's love and keep you strong. And may you have the power to understand, as all God's people should, how wide, how long, how high, and how deep his love is. May you experience the love of Christ, though it is too great to understand fully. Then you will be made complete with all the fullness of life and power that comes from God.

"Now all glory to God, who is able, through his mighty power at work within us, to accomplish infinitely more than we might ask or think. Glory to him in the church and in Christ Jesus through all generations forever and ever! Amen." (Paul, Ephesians 3:16–21)

One of my all-time favorite verses is Matthew 7:19–21:

"Do not store up for yourselves treasures here on earth, where moths can eat them and rust destroys them, and where thieves can break in and steal. Store your treasures in heaven, where moths and rust cannot destroy or thieves cannot break in and steal. For wherever your treasure is, there will your heart be also."

These verses brought about a whole new light and understanding showing me that the most important treasures we should adore and aim for are the ones that are remembered in heaven and the ones that bring us the greatest happiness and tears of joy here on earth. Treasures such as giving, caring and loving for the less fortunate, gentleness, kindness and compassion for everyone we come into contact with. Seeking out the gifts of the Spirit such as words of wisdom, faith, love, joy, peace and patience. And to constantly be looking at how we can be more like Christ…a Christian, in loving others with the love that Jesus has showered over us. The Bible is chock full of so many surprises and beautiful truths to guide you into a life of pure joy and unwavering faith. Truth that stands the test of time.

"Your eye is a lamp that provides light for your body. When your eye is good, your whole body is full of light. But when your eye is bad, your whole body is full of darkness. And if the light you think you have is actually darkness, how deep that darkness is! No one can serve two masters. For you will hate one and love the other; you will be devoted to one and despise the other. You cannot serve both God and Money." (Jesus, Matthew 6:22–24)

The war of wars is fought over the battle of greed and the sins of the flesh which we all fall to almost on a regular basis. Jesus is making it very clear here that those who believe in a "prosperous gospel" are wrong. I would have to strongly agree. The warnings of how the love of money can divide and be the destruction between you and Jesus is thoroughly described and forewarned in the Gospels as well as throughout the Bible.

In the Gospel of Luke 12:15 it says:

"Watch out! Be on your guard against all kinds of greed; a man's life does not consist in the abundance of his possessions." (Jesus)

"Whoever loves money never has enough; whoever loves wealth is never satisfied with their income. This too is meaningless." (Ecclesiastes 5:10)

"Better the little that the righteous have than the wealth of many wicked; for the power of the wicked will be broken, but the Lord upholds the righteous." (Psalm 37:16–17)

"Keep your lives free from the love of money and be content with what you have, because God has said, 'Never will I leave you; never will I forsake you.'" (Hebrews 13:5)

And finally,

"For the love of money is the root of all kinds of evil. And some people, craving money, have wandered from the true faith and pierced themselves with many sorrows." (Paul, 1 Timothy 6:10)

It is easy for us to simplify and justify our decisions and choices based on whatever story we choose to make up to explain away why it is okay to do what we do, knowing full well that it is wrong and full of sin. This is where the Holy Spirit steps in, quite regularly I might add, and actually disciplines us for our selfish actions and choices.

If we are to grow in our relationship with Christ, to fulfill our purpose for what we were created for, we need to simply comply and be obedient to the truths of God's word. He makes the things that we struggle with rather clear and straight to the point. "Just don't do it!" This is more clearly what I hear from the mouth of Jesus when I read the Gospels or any of the other books of the New Testament. I also believe we have lost touch as Christians to the depths of what Christ has truly called us to do.

"Pursue righteousness and a godly life, along with faith, love, perseverance, and gentleness. Fight the good fight for the true faith. Hold tightly to the eternal life to which God has called you, which you have confessed so well before many witnesses. And I charge you before God, who gives life to all, and before Christ Jesus, who gave a good testimony before Pontius Pilate, that you obey this command without wavering. Then no one can find fault with you from now until our Lord Jesus Christ comes again. For at just the right time Christ will be revealed from heaven by the blessed and only almighty God, the King of all kings and Lord of all lords." (Paul, 1 Timothy 6:11–15)

Before, during, and after the Civil War, there were many "Christians" who believed it was morally right to own slaves. Going so far as to fight to keep them. On the other side, there were Christians who were proclaiming the absolute opposite and fighting to change the perspective and open the minds of the blind to see clearly that this was not part of what Jesus proclaimed. But again, it more rightly came down to greed and the importance of their "property" being taken away from them that was more of their concern than to seek out what was morally correct. Freedom for slaves fell in line with the Gospels which fully explained the truths behind our Lord Jesus. They cared more about money, property and greed than living their lives for the sake of Christ.

"I live in a first-world country in the twenty-first century. And I am grateful for the freedoms and blessings I enjoy because of where and when I live. But when you're standing in an ancient catacomb, the comforts you enjoy make you uncomfortable. The things you complain about are convicting. And some of the sacrifices you've made for the cause of Christ might not even qualify under a second-century definition.

"As I tried to absorb the significance of where I was, I couldn't help but wonder if our generation has conveniently forgotten how inconvenient it can be to follow in the footsteps of Christ. I couldn't help but wonder if we have diluted the truths of Christianity and settled for superficialities. I couldn't help but wonder if we have accepted a form of Christianity that is more educated but less powerful, more civilized but less compassionate, more acceptable but less authentic than that which our spiritual ancestors practiced." (Mark Batterson, Primal)

I honestly believe that in the Bible…you can find the answers to almost any subject that you are currently struggling with in this life. It truly is the only life manual out there that can guide you and direct you to bring you peace and understanding, love and true forgiveness. Answers on how to live your life with peace and joy, contentment of your surroundings and possessions and fulfillment to the obedience of his truth which in turn brings you purpose, love, and the desires of your heart.

Life has been described in so many metaphors to simplify the challenges that we all face…it is almost endless. Life is a rollercoaster, life is trip, life is a journey, etc. I look to God's truths and wisdom to guide me, direct me and shine light into my heart and soul. We are all desperate to find love, peace and a true understanding of what all of this means. We are all looking for answers to help us understand how we do life, how we do marriage, parenting and finances. But most of all, we are looking for hope that is beyond this world and beyond the death that is imminent before us all.

"For God has not given us a spirit of fear and timidity, but of power, love and self-discipline. So never be ashamed to tell others about our Lord. And don't be ashamed of me, either, even though I'm in prison for him. With the strength God gives you, be ready to suffer with me for the sake of the Good News. For God saved us and called us to live a holy life. He did this not because we deserved it, but because that was his plan from before the beginning of time—to show us his grace through Christ Jesus. And now he has made all of this plain to us by the appearing of Christ Jesus, our Savior. He broke the power of death and illuminated the way to life and immortality through the Good News." (Paul, 2 Timothy 1:7–10)

The mysteries that Paul talks about throughout his letters are really no mystery at all once we have chosen to accept Christ as our Lord and Savior. Let me take a moment to give a greater detail in what it means to actually accept Christ into your heart.

When you make that choice, it is a choice of the utmost greatest importance. But it doesn't end there. All of us can say that Jesus is Lord of our lives and then turn around the next day and not act like it at all. Our free will is where we get to choose to either live it out or opt to be a hypocrite. To call him Lord is to proclaim he is the Lord over your life. That means you are choosing to surrender to his will in believing he can do a far greater job at directing your life than you ever will. It also means that you are a new creation, the old has gone and the new has come. This is where you begin the transformation of your life that is no longer yours but his. The Holy Spirit becomes bonded with your spirit and begins the life-long journey of transformation.

Trust, forgiveness, obedience, grace, and love start the amazing process of healing your brokenness, filling in all your cracks and putting *Neosporin* and *Band-Aids* on all of your "boo-boos" with which our heavenly Father kisses lovingly. But once you choose to become a child of God, don't be surprised if discipline comes your way, for your Father loves you so much that his discipline is a necessary step for your life to be made new, healthy, and to help steer you in the right direction for your life.

"And have you forgotten the encouraging words God spoke to you as his children? He said,

"'My child, don't make light of the Lord's discipline, and don't give up when he corrects you. For the Lord disciplines those he loves, and he punishes each one he accepts as his child.' (Proverbs 3:11–12)

"As you endure this divine discipline, remember that God is treating you as his own children. Who ever heard of a child who is never disciplined by its father? If God doesn't discipline you as he does all of his children, it means that you are illegitimate and are not really his children at all. Since we respected our earthly fathers who disciplined us, shouldn't we submit even more to the discipline of the Father of our spirits, and live forever?

"For our earthly fathers disciplined us for a few years, doing the best they knew how. But God's discipline is always good for us, so that we might share in his holiness. No discipline is enjoyable while it is happening—it's painful! But afterward there will be a peaceful harvest of right living for those who are trained in this way." (Hebrews 12:5-11)

As my favorite Christian band, *MercyMe*, says in one of their songs, "It's all about the change!"

When you break it all down…it comes down to a choice. God has given you the gift of free will and the freedom to choose your own destiny. The freedom to choose whatever it is you choose to believe. But he doesn't leave you hanging there without knowing full well the results of your choices. He gives us ample time in each of our lives to survey the evidence and to seek out the truth, solve the mystery and unveil the secrets of life, love, and the pursuit of happiness. The warnings are self-evident. You reap what you sow. Karma, some may say, comes back hard to bite us in the behind.

We are creatures who are stubborn and bull-headed to no end, but Jesus knew this and experienced it firsthand at the hands of his own disciples, accusers and executioners. We want to fight the truth and not have to bend to its will on our lives, even if it is for our benefit. We will fight for the belief, which is a lie, that we can do life better and without God's guidance or the saving grace and forgiveness of Jesus Christ. Why? Because we believe somewhere deep down that we are god. We have control over our lives and we know ourselves better than anyone else…even better than the one who created us.

Let me just be real here for a moment. Every single one of us is a hypocrite to some degree, including me, but the beautiful and unfathomable grace of God always steps in and says, "I love you anyway." And that right there is the Good News of Jesus Christ.

We like to say to ourselves, and to some point even believe, we can do life better without God. *"I know what it is that is going to make me happy and what it is that I need most. I know what I need to do and where I need to go. Therefore, I am in charge of me, nobody else."* Until we fall flat on our faces in utter despair, tears falling everywhere and then we ask, *"Why God? Why me? What did I do to deserve this?"* In which God replies, *"I didn't do this to you, you did. You made the choice to go your own way, without me. I have made myself known to you. I reached out to you through your friends who told you about me. I have not hidden anything from you. My creation is all around you in plain sight so that you would know how much I love you by providing everything you need. I even sent my only Son as a sacrifice for your poor choices, your addictions, your habits and sins of the flesh. I have done everything for you but you chose to say "No" to my free gift of salvation and eternal life. And, I even wrapped up all the truth and wisdom you would need in a beautiful little package called the Bible."*

The craziest thing of all and what I think is still the greatest mystery is that no matter what you have done, no matter how many times you fail, or how many times you fall or screw up, no matter what kind of life you have chosen to live, Jesus loves you just the same and he loves you right where you sit. You cannot ever do anything to the point of him loving you less or him abandoning you for your poor choices. ***He will never leave you***…plain and simple. He has done everything required to be pronounced our Lord and Savior. If we would only set our egos and selfishness aside and choose to accept and follow him.

Sadly, many of us will not choose Jesus. We will instead choose to believe that we have control and that we, ourselves, know better. We repeatedly have gone so far as to mock Jesus, Christianity, and the faith of God to the point of kicking him out of every part of our lives. We have, as the human race, exhumed him from all points of interest and are heading exactly in the direction that Jesus proclaimed and prophesied over two thousand years ago.

"Then you will be arrested, persecuted and killed. You will be hated all over the world because you are my followers. And many will turn away from me and betray and hate each other. Sin will be rampant everywhere, and the love of many will grow cold. But the one who endures to the end will be saved." (Jesus, Matthew 24:9–10, 12)

The cross is one of the most brutal and heinous tortures of death ever created by man. But yet, the symbol of the cross is widely known for the representation of the deep love and forgiveness that is found there. It is the only symbol of torture that we see not as death, or evil…but a symbol of love, hope, and life after death. It is the only hope for mankind and yet we are trying everything in our power to distinguish it from our lives in every way possible. Just out of curiosity…have you or anyone else ever seen a necklace with an electric chair or the symbol of a noose hanging around someone's neck to proclaim love? I didn't think so.

God's mysterious plan is quite simply the most beautiful story ever told. He created us and with our free will, we chose sin and death over eternal life. God loved the world so much that he sent his only Son to redeem us in our relationship to the Father so that we could have a second chance at making a better choice. To choose life and live it fully…to choose Jesus, full of redemption, healing, love and forgiveness. A chance to live a life full of joy and happiness. A reliance on a God who loves us and wants to show us a better way. There are no promises that there will not be pain and suffering but there will be hope and trust, truth and light. For this life is a short while…but eternity is forever. I choose life, I choose love and I choose eternity with the only one who truly loves me just as I am.

"What we do see is Jesus, and because he suffered death for us, he is now 'crowned with glory and honor.' Yes, by God's grace, Jesus tasted death for everyone. God, for whom and through whom everything was made, chose to bring many children into glory. And it was only right that he should make Jesus, through his suffering, a perfect leader, fit to bring them into their salvation.

"So now Jesus and the ones he makes holy have the same Father. That is why Jesus is not ashamed to call them his brothers and sisters.

"Because God's children are human beings—made of flesh and blood—the Son also became flesh and blood. For only as a human being could he die, and only by dying could he break the power of the devil, who had the power of death. Only in this way could he set free all who have lived their lives as slaves to the fear of dying." (Hebrews 2:9–15)

"In the beginning the Word [Jesus] already existed. The Word was with God, and the Word was God. He existed in the beginning with God. God created everything through him, and nothing was created except through him. The Word gave life to everything that was created, and his life brought light to everyone. The light shines in the darkness, and the darkness can never extinguish it." (John 1:1–5)

"Without question, this is the greatest mystery of our faith: Christ was revealed in a human body and vindicated by the Spirit. He was seen by angels and announced to the nations. He was believed in throughout the world and taken to heaven in glory." (Paul, 1 Timothy 3:16)

"It occurs to me that all the contorted theories about Jesus that have been spontaneously generating since the day of his death merely confirm the awesome risk God took when he stretched himself out on the dissection table—a risk he seemed to welcome. Examine me. Test me. You decide." (Philip Yancey, *The Jesus I Never Knew*)

Chapter 7

The Healings

"After Jesus left the girl's home, two blind men followed along behind him, shouting, 'Son of David, have mercy on us!' They went right into the house where he was staying, and Jesus asked them, 'Do you believe I can make you see?'

"'Yes, Lord,' they told him, 'we do.' Then he touched their eyes and said, 'Because of your faith, it will happen.' Then their eyes were opened, and they could see!"

—Matthew 9:27–30

"He personally carried our sins in his body on the cross so that we can be dead to sin and live for what is right. By his wounds you have been healed."

—1 Peter 2:24

As a kid, I was extremely fascinated with the healings of Jesus and often wondered how that kind of impact affected the lives of those who received such gifts with compassion and love. I have often tried to imagine what it would have been like, sitting on the sidelines, watching Jesus performing miracle after miracle for everyone to see and marvel at. The reactions to the healings that were taking place must have been an awe-inspiring and extremely dramatic experience. The miracles most likely would have been followed by sounds of absolute inquisitive surprise, and complete amazement.

In Jesus's three-year ministry, he healed hundreds if not thousands of people. It has always been one of my goals to discuss and highlight some of the more defining moments of the healings that took place from this ordinary Jew, a carpenter by trade. When he would compassionately and lovingly stop whatever he was doing to change someone's life dramatically through a miraculous healing, by just the touch of his hand or a simple word, the impact of that healing emphatically did so much more to the people he encountered and even to those who were witnesses.

In all, there is no way to actually count how many people Jesus healed, which ones he touched, which ones touched him or if he even went to see them at all, but instead chose to heal them from a distance, with just a few words. The miracles of Jesus are simply hard for us to fathom because it is completely out of our realm of normalcy as it was in the time that Jesus was walking amongst us. I do believe, however, that miracles do happen every day. Just not to the magnitude as we read of in the Gospels. Nor do we hear of the dramatic fashion in which Jesus constantly blew their minds with his authority and ability to direct such super powers at his own free will.

Just to be clear here, I am not going to try and convince you that these events truly took place because that is not my intention. I will make a claim right here and now that every one of these miracles, I believe, without a doubt, did happen exactly the way they have been told to us in the four Gospels. I also believe in the power of prayer and that faith is still just as powerful now as it was even then. We must simply TRUST and BELIEVE.

About six months prior to writing this book, I carefully read through the four Gospels and I decided I wanted to jot down all the miracles and healings of Jesus just to absorb the volume of Jesus's work. My goal was to focus on a few of the more impactful stories of the healings and the people that were wrapped up in them. To me, they represent a huge part of Jesus's ministry as he proved to be the healer for every part of our misery and struggle in this often difficult life. He healed the physical, the mental, the emotional and the spiritual parts of our existence. Most of them are unnamed folks who sought him out to relieve their discomfort, their pain, their sickness, their demons, their disease and their lack of faith and loneliness.

No one has ever touched the hearts of people in the way that Jesus did and that is just one of a thousand different reasons as to why I am even writing this book about him. It is quite possible this is the same reason you chose to pick up this book and are reading about him as well.

Throughout the four Gospels, I counted 68 times that Jesus either performed a miracle or there was a healing taking place. Most of the time, the healings that are being mentioned are in one town, in a synagogue, or in one sitting. Jesus moved from town to town and had compassion on everyone he came into contact with. Never once did he deny healing or love but accepted everyone as friends. Even as exhausted as he was most of the time he gave continuously to all who approached him with open arms.

Of the different styles of the four writers of the four Gospels, Luke's Gospel is the one I sincerely enjoy the most. His complete and thorough journalism and examination through the process of gathering all the information, descriptions, and details of the events, people, and places is so good that it easily paints a complete picture of the testimony that is being mapped out about this man, Jesus, and I just love reading about it.

In chapter 3, Luke makes it very clear as to when in our history, Jesus comes into his glory and begins his ministry and the purpose for why he came to earth in the flesh to live amongst us, even though he is the Son of God.

Here is how Luke chapter 3 begins:

"It was now the fifteenth year of the reign of Tiberius, the Roman emperor. Pontius Pilate was governor over Judea; Herod Antipas was ruler over Galilee; his brother Philip was ruler over Iturea and Traconitis; Lysanias was ruler over Abilene. Annas and Caiaphas were the high priests." (Luke 3:1–2)

If my knowledge of history serves me correctly, this would put the time frame right around 27–30 AD.

In the fourth chapter of Luke, verse 14, Jesus is returning to Nazareth ready to begin his ministry, proclaiming himself the Messiah foretold of in the book of Isaiah…

"The blind see, the lame walk, the lepers are cured, the deaf hear, the dead are raised to life and the Good News is being preached to the poor." (Matthew 11:5)

"Then Jesus returned to Galilee, filled with the Holy Spirit's power. Reports about him spread quickly through the whole region. He taught regularly in their synagogues and was praised by everyone.

"When he came to the village of Nazareth, his boyhood home, he went as usual to the synagogue on the Sabbath and stood up to read the Scriptures. "The scroll of Isaiah the prophet was handed to him. He unrolled the scroll and found the place where this was written:

"'The Spirit of the Lord is upon me,
for he has anointed me to bring Good News to the poor.
He has sent me to proclaim that captives will be released,

125

that the blind will see,
that the oppressed will be set free,
and that the time of the Lord's favor has come.'"
(Isaiah 61:1–2)

"He rolled up the scroll, handed it back to the attendant, and sat down. All eyes in the synagogue looked at him intently. Then he began to speak to them. 'The Scripture you've just heard has been fulfilled this very day!'" (Luke 4:14–21)

Whoa! Wait a minute. Can you even visualize for a second, after hearing this proclamation, how thick the drama must have been, the intensity, and the curiosity of what just took place inside this synagogue? This shocking statement must have left them standing there completely perplexed, while looking at this man, Jesus, questioning in their minds and asking themselves, "Did he just say what I think he said?" Everyone in that synagogue had already heard reports about Jesus. But now here he stands before them, having just read from the book of Isaiah and he is proclaiming himself to be the Christ? The fulfillment of this very prophesy? This was the son of Joseph and Mary from this very town where he grew up as a boy. Everyone knew him and his entire family. How could this boy, this ordinary man, a carpenter, be the Messiah?

"Where does he get this wisdom and the power to do miracles?' Then they scoffed, 'He's just the carpenter's son, and we know Mary, his mother, and his brothers—James, Joseph, Simon and Judas. All his sisters live right here among us. Where did he learn all these things?' And they were deeply offended and refused to believe in him." (Matthew 13:54–57)

But Jesus did not hesitate to proclaim his messiahship as soon as his time had come. And he certainly did not proclaim it in the shadows or behind closed doors. He went right to the synagogue, found just one of the prophecies that were told about him in the book of Isaiah and laid it all out there for everyone to see.

He quite conclusively backed up his claim as the Messiah with so many miracles and healings but also through the wisdom of his teaching. One would have to assume, after listening to his sermons and parables that he had to have been brought up under the wings of a Rabbi who exclusively taught him the Torah anticipating his future role as a competent religious leader.

"Then Jesus went to Capernaum, a town in Galilee, and taught there in the synagogue every Sabbath day. There, too, the people were amazed at his teaching, for he spoke with authority.

"Once when he was in the synagogue, a man possessed by a demon—an evil spirit—began shouting at Jesus, 'Go away! Why are you interfering with us Jesus of Nazareth? Have you come to destroy us? I know who you are—the Holy One of God!'

"Jesus cut him short. 'Be quiet! Come out of the man,' he ordered. At that, the demon threw the man to the floor as the crowd watched; then it came out of him without hurting him further.

"Amazed, the people exclaimed, 'What authority and power this man's words possess! Even evil spirits obey him, and they flee at his command!' The news about Jesus spread through every village in the entire region." (Luke 4:31–37)

Later that same day, after Jesus left the synagogue....

"As the sun went down that evening, people throughout the village brought sick family members to Jesus. No matter what their diseases were, the touch of his hand healed every one. Many were possessed by demons, and the demons came out at his command, shouting, 'You are the Son of God!' But because they knew he was the Messiah, he rebuked them and refused to let them speak." (Luke 4:40–41)

It is amazing to think that just the touch of Jesus's hand, or even just a word from his mouth healed every one and every single disease, *"no matter what their diseases were,"* that were brought before him. And again, we are told that he cast out demons who proclaimed his identity as Jesus, the Son of God. This truth alone gives me so much hope and encouragement, knowing full well that he has already conquered the evil of this world.

I would like for you to think about this for a moment. How reassuring and comforting is it to know that he has such power over the demons and even Satan himself? Silencing them every time they wanted to speak out and proclaim who Jesus truly was.

I would like to take a few minutes to emphasize the importance of the healings that took place in the form of exorcisms that Jesus came across quite regularly and the reassuring fact that we are safe in the hands of Jesus.

Throughout the Gospels, one of the things that I read which completely fascinated me was how Jesus did not want the demons to proclaim the truth of his identity. The demons would be shouting out loud that he was the "Son of God" or the "Holy One of God" but Jesus silenced them and kept them from pointing out the obvious. I wonder why he did not want them to proclaim his deity. Who better to claim his true identity than his number one enemy?

I personally have not had a lot of experience in the realm of darkness, demon possession or things of this kind. I have done my best to stay away from anything that remotely resembles something evil, satanic or has to do with the occult. But there was one time, just out of plain youthful curiosity, that I tried using a *Ouija* board with a couple of friends while in middle school. Not really believing that this "game" could possibly have any coincidence or legitimacy to a supernatural evil or that it could actually even be a tool for the devil…but I was wrong.

With the three of us all putting two fingers on the triangular piece sitting atop the board, we asked it a couple of questions and not a few seconds later it started to move…on its own, I kid you not! If you're not familiar with this, good, don't be.

One of my friends that I was with had an older sister and no one knew where she was. So we decided to ask the *Ouija* board where she was and what time would she be home? The triangular piece moved to some numbers and then it moved to a couple of letters. I can't be sure if they were in exact order but I do remember 6, 3, 0 then the letters U and W.

Well, it was already freaking me out that this triangular piece was even moving by itself, but even freakier than that was the next day, we found out that my friend's sister came home at the exact time it was predicted, 6:30 p.m. and the *Ouija* board even told us where she had been, UW (University of Washington). Freaky!

The moral of the story is: don't play with things that are not meant to be played with. Don't even think of messing around with the occult or anything of that kind. You will get burned. The spiritual realm of darkness is very real and I believe God keeps a pretty firm grasp on not allowing it to affect or penetrate us in any such way unless an individual chooses to personally seek it out.

Throughout my life I have heard of many different stories from different pastors who personally had to confront and deal with people who were actually demon possessed and let me tell you…their stories are rather frightening.

I did have one experience I will never forget which I do believe was an encounter of demon possession, although I cannot confirm it.

I was riding a school bus up a hill out of a housing complex called Riverbend in the town of North Bend where I grew up. At the top of this hill was a young man, probably in his early twenties, who had his back to all of the kids that were on the bus while we were stopped at a stop sign. As you can imagine, a majority of the kids who were looking out the window of this bus were quite inquisitive as to why this man was standing by himself at a stop sign. He was hunched over, shoulders slouched with long, greasy hair that was all messed up and ratted. His clothes were dirty with holes in various places and as it was typical for this era, he only wore a T-shirt and jeans.

As soon as we came to a stop at the top of this hill, with all eyes on him, he quickly turned around and shrieked at us with an evil scream while forming satanic signs with his hands. We all jumped back in shock and could even hear a few screams as we were completely perplexed by this man and his wicked demeanor.

Looking back on this now and at many times throughout my life, he easily resembled the creature, Gollum, from the Lord of the Rings, who was possessed by the evil of that ring. The screech and look of this man, especially in his eyes, was both terrifying and interesting at the same time. With absolute curiosity, we stared at him continuously as we proceeded to move forward and down the hill.

He too, never lost eye contact with us as he swiveled his head without moving his body following the movement of the bus as it turned to go down the hill. He never once stopped staring us down, hunched over with the look of death and destruction in his eyes. It was altogether a very real and scary scene.

Back in the late seventies and the early eighties, as I was attending youth group at our church, there were many things being shared with us that opened our eyes and ears to the darkness and evil that was present even in the music we were listening to. Totally unaware at this time that the devil was clearly in the lyrics of songs even if those lyrics didn't make sense.

If you are not familiar with back masking, it is something that scared the daylights out of me when it was shown to me so many years ago as a teenager in youth group. Since then, it has long since fallen by the way side and I don't believe it is even a subject that is talked about these days. I was never sure if it was accurate or even legit, but it was definitely scary to hear.

Back masking is a recording technique in which a sound, message or lyrics are recorded backward onto a track that is meant to be played forward. But the scariest part was when a song was sung and recorded normally, but while being played backward had hidden messages within it that were quite evil and very dark. Which I believe, many times, was also a process, in which a message was found through phonetic reversal but was unintentional.

For example, when a song was played backward, either by rotating a record in the opposite direction or by other means, you can hear clearly, in some instances, messages within those lyrics and most of those messages contained evil sayings, directions or words. It literally brought goosebumps and the raising of the hair on the back of my neck. Simply frightening!

I will have to admit that some of the messages were very compelling and if true, were downright freaky. I never tried it myself to see if it would work, but if so, I don't see this being a coincidence. I believe the devil has many tricks up his sleeve and will use many different angles and subjects like music, movies, internet, games and books, to get your attention away from God so he can plant in your brain the things HE wants you to see or hear.

The less you think about Jesus, the less constructive you will be in serving and loving God and others. The father of lies is very good at deceiving us, tempting us, and drawing us away, to fall and fail once again. The more we fail, the more we will feel helpless and hopeless in our ability to be affective in being God's witnesses in serving others with the love of Jesus Christ.

In all, I do believe that music, and the influence it has on us, is far deeper than we can possibly imagine. Many will dispute this claim because we take our music very seriously and nobody wants to hear this truth. Most of the secular music out there is not hiding what they are promoting or displaying in the art work of their albums or even more clearly, being sung in the lyrics of their songs. If you are listening to *AC/DC's CD, "Highway to Hell,"* there is a pretty good chance that the lyrics of their songs are pushing you to live in such a way as to eventually arrive on that particular highway…which would not be a destination I would want to arrive at in any form or fashion.

Most of the lyrics in the songs the artists are choosing to sing is the kind of material that sells. It is also revealing truthfully where their heart is, their beliefs in God or not, and if they even care. They know full well that this world is in utter chaos within the realms of loneliness, drugs, full blown sex of every kind, depression, greed and pure destructiveness. So why wouldn't it sell? They are simply feeding into what is already present in so many hearts, souls, and minds, of many, many people both young and old, who are living in the depths of darkness and sin.

Thank God for Jesus and his loving and healing Spirit, who continually reveals his love, patience, mercy, and grace, on a world so deep in sin and darkness.

I have always been drawn to the themes of love, forgiveness, equality, and compassion in music. Don't get me wrong, I still attended quite a few rock concerts throughout my life like *Van Halen, Def Leppard* (three times, they were my favorite) and singers like *Tom Petty, Bruce Springsteen,* and *Madonna,* but I knew there were limits and I also knew I had to protect my heart. Needless to say, I am still stuck in the eighties. I love eighties music, but I have moved on to some of the most incredible and inspirational Christian artists such as *MercyMe, Third Day, Toby Mac,* and *Lauren Daigle. MercyMe,* hands down, is easily my favorite. Anyway…let's get back to the subject matter.

In Luke chapter 5, there is a story of healing that has always been one of my favorites to read and ponder. It is a story of a man with an advanced case of leprosy. If you are not familiar with leprosy, let me give you some back story on this disease and the crippling affect it has on the lives that it touches.

One of the most well-known examples of a debilitating disease is Mycobacterium leprae, the infectious bacterial agent of leprosy. Leprosy is discussed quite often in the bible. While its definition in modern times is different from biblical times, there is no doubt that the definitions over-lap, and the modern form of the disease (Hansen's disease), still illustrates important spiritual lessons for today.

The term "leprosy" (including leper, lepers, leprosy, leprous) occurs 68 times in the bible—55 times in the Old Testament and 13 times in the New Testament. In the Old Testament, the instances of leprosy most likely meant a variety of infectious skin diseases, and even mold and mil-dew on clothing and walls. The precise meaning of the leprosy in both the Old and New Testaments is still in dispute, but it probably includes the modern Hansen's disease (especially in the New Testament) and infectious skin diseases.

Studying leprosy helps us to see why pain is a valuable "gift."

The term "Hansen's disease" was not given until 1873, when Gerhard Henrik Armauer Hansen described the leprosy bacillus (the lay term for the "bacterium"). Only at this point was a precise definition for leprosy made available.

Leprosy has terrified humanity since ancient times and was reported as early as 600 B.C. in India, China, and Egypt. For many centuries, leprosy was considered a curse of God, often associated with sin. It did not kill, but neither did it seem to end. Instead, it lingered for years, causing the tissues to degenerate and deforming the body.

Many have thought leprosy to be a disease of the skin. It is better classified, however, as a disease of the nervous system because the leprosy bacterium attacks the nerves. Leprosy is spread by multiple contacts, as well as by droplets from the respiratory tracts, such as nasal secretions that are transmitted from person to person.

Its symptoms start in the skin and peripheral nervous system, then spread to other parts, such as the hands, feet, face, and earlobes. Patients with leprosy experience disfigurement of the skin and bones, twisting of the limbs, and curling of the fingers to form the characteristic claw hand. Facial changes include thickening of the outer ear and collapsing of the nose.

The largest number of deformities develop from loss of pain sensation due to extensive nerve damage. It was the work of Dr. Paul Brand (the late world-renowned orthopedic surgeon and leprosy physician) with leprosy patients that illustrated, in part, the value of sensing pain in this world. The leprosy bacillus destroys nerve endings that carry pain signals; therefore patients with advanced leprosy experience a total loss of physical pain. When these people cannot sense touch or pain, they tend to injure themselves or be unaware of injury caused by an outside agent.

In fact, some leprosy patients have had their fingers eaten by rats in their sleep because they were totally unaware of it happening; the lack of pain receptors could not warn them of the danger.

In addition to pain and disfiguration, biblical leprosy and Hansen's disease are both dreaded, and people were shunned because of them. References to leprosy have a different emphasis in the New Testament. They stress God's desire to heal. Jesus freely touched people with leprosy. While people with leprosy traditionally suffered banishment from family and neighbors, Jesus broke from the tradition. He treated lepers with compassion, touching and healing them.

Studying leprosy helps us see why pain is a valuable "gift," a survival mechanism to warn us of danger in this world. Without pain and suffering, we might be lepers, unable to recognize that something is terribly wrong and that we need the healing touch of God.

As Dr. Brand said, 'I cannot think of a greater gift that I could give my leprosy patients than pain.' (Dr. Alan L. Gillen, *Answers Magazine*)

As you can see, leprosy is not only a debilitating disease but a life-long death sentence that seems to never end. In Luke chapter 5,

Jesus does something that no one else, not then, and certainly not even today, would dare to do…he reaches out and touches a leper.

"In one of the villages, Jesus met a man with an advanced case of leprosy. When the man saw Jesus, he bowed with his face to the ground (most likely because of the disfiguration of his skin and face) begging to be healed. 'Lord,' he said, 'if you are willing, you can heal me and make me clean.'

Jesus reached out and touched him. 'I am willing,' he said. 'Be healed!' And instantly the leprosy disappeared." (Luke 5:12–13, emphasis mine)

This solemn act of kindness, love and compassion is unmatched in the realm of our humanity today. The act of touching him while healing him was more deeply received by the leper than we could possibly understand or fathom.

We get a glimpse into the extremely decrepit, hopeless and lonely life of this man in just a few facts through these verses. One, his leprosy is in the advanced stage, letting us know that most likely he has had this disease for quite some time if not for many, many years. Two, he bowed with his face to the ground, giving us a hint that he was ashamed so as to not even look Jesus in the eyes while begging to be healed and made clean. Three, he goes so far as to say, "*if you are willing*" which implies he has nothing to lose and is reaching out to Jesus because this man knows Jesus is his last hope for healing. And finally, the leper doesn't just ask for healing but to also be made clean again, which I believe would imply giving him, once again, a normal life from all the sickness, disease, deformity, loneliness, and banishment that he has had to live with for far too long.

I instantly think of my own life and how incredibly saddening that would be to feel banished from your own family because of a disease that threatened everyone in close proximity. It hasn't been that long ago when AIDS and HIV threatened our very existence essentially labeling people with a huge sign around their neck that read "Unclean" before finding out that this disease is not transmittable through the air or from normal physical contact. This disease quickly became known as the "Gay disease" and with that stigma was given a receipt of death.

I remember how almost instantly this plague was wrapped up in and titled as a discriminative, debilitating act of God against those who chose to live a homosexual lifestyle and for those who had drug addictions which involved needles and syringes. And because it was transmittable by body fluids and blood, this category of men was suffering a great loss in numbers due to their current lifestyles and sexual orientation. But let me say this: If Jesus had been born and was living out his ministry now, just as he did two thousand years ago, at this particular time, I have no doubt at all he would have healed these men from their diseases and in their distress, without blinking an eye. His love and compassion for them would have been the same, and still is, as it was for Mary Magdelene, whose sins were many in her profession as a prostitute.

Jesus loves EVERYONE, no matter what sin they have committed, are committing, or through whatever lifestyle they have chosen. And in my opinion, from all my studies, from all my experiences of God's love and mercy on my life and from what I have come to understand of the love of Jesus through his example and his words, to simply clarify that one sin is greater than another is absolutely preposterous. No ONE is without sin! Judge not so you will not be judged!

As I think of this story and the overwhelming compassion Jesus had for this man with leprosy, and so many others, I can't help to think of the ramifications of this one healing and the aftermath of joy and acceptance this man had the chance to feel and experience once again. Maybe he had children or a wife that he could go back home to and be with once again. To hug them, touch them and love them with no shame or fear. Imagine the depth of love, acceptance, and reassurance of your life filled with once again with affection and love renewed in a life that was hopeless and so alone. A dead man walking but made new again.

Lepers were not only shunned, people literally ran away from them. And lepers were forced to yell "unclean, unclean" everywhere they went. The isolation alone would have been enough suffering to have caused a man or woman to fold up, die, and wither away.

We don't know any of the backstory of this man whose life was drastically changed by just the touch of Jesus's hand. And we have no indication as to what took place after the healing other than the fact that he could not keep it a secret as Jesus asked him to do.

"Then Jesus instructed him not to tell anyone what had happened. He said, 'Go to the priest and let him examine you. Take along the offering required in the law of Moses for those who have been healed of leprosy. This will be a public testimony that you have been cleansed.'

"But despite Jesus's instructions, the report of his power spread even faster, and vast crowds came to hear him preach and to be healed of their diseases. But Jesus often withdrew to the wilderness for prayer." (Luke 5:14–16)

This, of course, is just one example of the impact of healings that Jesus performed in front of everyone. Not ever shying away from revealing his true identity as the prophesied Messiah, he healed literally thousands of people on his journeys from city to city and town to town. But this one story always struck a chord in my heart to the depths of his love for us to even go so far as touching a man who is covered in a very easily transmittable skin disease.

Sadly, the man may have not even felt the touch of Jesus as his nerve endings and receptors most assuredly had been extremely damaged. But I am guessing the opposite. I would even presume that the moment Jesus laid his hand on him was the moment he was instantly flooded with the intense power of healing throughout his whole body, from the top of his head to every new fingertip that was being replaced all the way to the tips of his toes that might have been missing. Goose bumps rising in succession as every ounce of his body is cleansed of dried dead skin, boils, cracks, and deformities made whole. His entire body thriving with sensation and of feeling, being made new once again. Can you even fathom how that must have felt for this diseased and hopeless man?

Imagine for a second, every cell and every layer of skin, repaired and made new in an instant. His face repaired with zero deformities, fresh and made clean. What a sight to behold and what a joy to have experienced the Lord's healing power even at the microbiological level. Simply amazing!

This is just a foreshadow of all that Jesus wants to give us. His compassion, love, and generosity await in anticipation of us, his creation, to simply say yes to the ultimate forgiveness and love through the blood that was shed on the cross for us.

One of the other things that I have pondered is what it must have been like for his disciples to watch and witness these things taking place, miracles and healings, a man dead for four days rising out of the grave still wrapped in his linens with a stench of death still wafting through the air. The crashing seas and swift and brutal winds stopping at the command of the commander, with just one word, nature even listens to his firm demands. Peter longs to have faith enough to step out of the boat into the elements and join Jesus as he is standing firmly on liquid H_2O, breaking all natural laws to exemplify his title as Son of God!

"Then Jesus got into the boat and started across the lake with his disciples. Suddenly, a fierce storm struck the lake, with waves breaking into the boat. But Jesus was sleeping. The disciples went and woke him up, shouting, 'Lord, save us! We're going to drown!'

"Jesus responded, 'Why are you afraid? You have so little faith!' Then he got up and rebuked the wind and the waves, and suddenly there was a great calm.

"The disciples were amazed, 'Who is this man?' they asked. 'Even the winds and waves obey him!'" (Matthew 8:23–27)

I almost wonder if these things became unimpressive as the days and years passed with each additional healing or miracle that was being exposed to them almost on a daily basis. And you have to at least imagine for a moment that if the waves were breaking into the boat that it must have been thrashing around in the water and the wind with a sea-sickening effect. Either way, Jesus was a very deep sleeper or he was completely exhausted. I am guessing the latter.

"Soon afterward Jesus went with his disciples to the village of Nain, and a large crowd followed him. A funeral procession was coming out as he approached the village gate. The young man who had died was a widow's only son, and a large crowd from the village was with her. When the Lord saw her, his heart overflowed with compassion. "Don't cry!" he said. Then he walked over to the coffin and touched it and the bearers stopped. 'Young man,' he said. 'I tell you, get up.' Then the dead boy sat up and began to talk! And Jesus gave him back to his mother." (Luke 7:11-15)

In this story, and if I am reading it correctly, Jesus doesn't even touch the child physically, he touches the coffin. Jesus's healing touch moved through the fibers and DNA of the wood the coffin was made of and into this young man, bringing him back to life. How awesome is that?

To have been a bystander or a follower watching Jesus do all these things must have been a mind boggling experience. Most of the Jewish nation was in turmoil over their poverty from being taxed so heavily by the Romans, watching, pillaging and ruling their every move. To have a prophet arrive in their presence and perform the miracles that Jesus did must have given them a sense of hope they had been longing for, waiting for…praying for. Hope and excitement was in the air as huge crowds would follow and watch his every move.

One of these bystanders was a woman, Mary Magdalene, who I mentioned earlier was a prostitute. In these verses from Luke, chapter 7, Mary takes a huge risk in entering the house of a Pharisee knowing full well how these Pharisees feel about her. She knows that she is unclean, a sinner and someone who is not welcome in their home, but she decides to push through with incredible courage to give to Jesus all that she has and shower him with her love, her actions, and appreciation for what he has done for her.

"One of the Pharisees asked Jesus to have dinner with him, so Jesus went to his home and sat down to eat." (Luke 7:36)

(Side note here: Most, if not all of the Pharisees and religious leaders, were planning and continually looking for opportunities to catch Jesus in something that could be used against him so they could arrest him and crucify him.)

"When a certain immoral woman from that city heard he was eating there, she brought a beautiful alabaster jar filled with expensive perfume. Then she knelt behind him at his feet, weeping. Her tears fell on his feet, and she wiped them off with her hair. Then she kept kissing his feet and putting perfume on them." (Luke 7:37–38)

Can you find a more beautiful sentiment in the actions of this remorseful and grateful woman who fully understood, in her stature, and in her situation, what Jesus truly meant to her and even more so, what Jesus's presence has already done for her? She has already, in one way or another, felt the overwhelming hope and forgiveness in the grace and love of this man who is spilling and overflowing with compassion and kindness to everyone who comes in contact with him. Either in his healings, his sermons, his feeding of the five thousand or raising children from the dead, his compassion, hope, love and kindness has revealed something very special. To all who have come into contact or for those who have personally experienced his healing touch, he was making monstrous waves in the lives of many.

These elements are gold. These are treasure...held in the hearts of millions if not billions of people around the world...hoping and praying for mercy and grace on all of us...sinners. This is what Mary Magdalene felt in her heart and she could not sit by and do nothing. She had to show her appreciation and love for Jesus because of the way he made her feel and because she knew her sins had been forgiven. She was made whole again, a new creation, her guilt and shame were no longer a part of her identity. I, personally, have experienced this transformation through the love and forgiveness of Christ. I still to this day, almost every time I am in church worshiping Jesus, cry tears of joy and thankfulness for the redeeming power of Christ in my heart and in my life. I cannot, like Mary, sit by and do nothing. The love of Jesus in my life is overwhelmingly beautiful and he deserves my life and my praise.

"When the Pharisee who had invited him saw this, he said to himself, 'If this man were a prophet, he would know what kind of woman is touching him. She's a sinner!'"

"Then Jesus answered his thoughts. 'Simon,' he said to the Pharisee, 'I have something to say to you.'

"Go ahead, Teacher,' Simon replied.

"Then Jesus told him this story: 'A man loaned money to two people—500 pieces of silver to one and 50 pieces to the other. But neither of them could repay him, so he kindly forgave them both, canceling their debts. Who do you suppose loved him more after that?'

"Simon answered, 'I suppose the one for whom he canceled the larger debt.'

"That's right,' Jesus said. Then he turned to the woman and said to Simon, 'Look at this woman kneeling here. When I entered your home, you didn't offer me water to wash the dust from my feet, but she has washed them with her tears and wiped them with her hair. You didn't greet me with a kiss, [which was a proper thing to do back then as a sign of respect] but from the time I first came in, she has not stopped kissing my feet. You neglected the courtesy of olive oil to anoint my head, but she has anointed my feet with rare perfume.

"I tell you, her sins—and they are many—have been forgiven, so she has showed me much love. But a person who is forgiven little shows only little love.' Then Jesus said to the woman, 'Your sins are forgiven.'

"The men at the table said among themselves, 'Who is this man that he goes around forgiving sins?'

"And Jesus said to the woman, 'Your faith has saved you; go in peace.'" (Jesus, Luke 7:39–50, emphasis mine)

This story, like so many others, is a story of unconditional and unwavering love overflowing with compassion, concern, grace, mercy and forgiveness. Jesus completely changed the game with a fresh presence of spiritual empathy that surrounds us, heals us and gives us a pure and thorough embrace unlike no other we could ever receive or imagine. I absolutely love the way Jesus is able to get his very important points across in the stories and parables he is telling. He explains very simply and carefully to the men (and especially Simon, the Pharisee,) the situation standing right in front of them in the example of this dear woman. She simply wants to show Jesus her love, gratitude and appreciation for who he truly is and what he has done for her already just by his actions and words.

She loves him passionately to the point of weeping, kneeling at his feet kissing them and pouring perfume on them and wiping his feet with her hair. I almost wonder if she knew already that his feet were going to be pierced brutally by a huge nail in the near future at his crucifixion. The aroma of that place, filled with perfume, grateful tears and a love so overwhelming, and yet, the Pharisees could see nothing but a sinner, unclean, touching Jesus. A woman who they believed to be a worthless human being, not worthy of an ounce of their time, love, or acceptance. Because of their blindness they could not understand the elegance of this woman redeemed by Jesus, showering him with her love and tears but also, in their blindness, could not see clearly that Jesus was, and still is, the true Messiah.

I would like to discuss two more stories of Jesus's healings if I may. It is obviously difficult to cover all the miracles and healings, but I would like to talk about each of the healings and what I have found to be simply beautiful.

Almost every healing of Jesus was brought upon by the faith of the one being healed or from a father or mother of a child who is very sick or who has died. Of course, Jesus's compassion for everyone who he personally came into contact with was a no brainer and you just knew that healing was not far behind.

I believe that when Jesus healed someone, he wanted to make sure that it didn't go just skin deep. In every situation where healing took place, I believe Jesus not only healed the physical ailment of each particular patient but even more so to the depths of their entire body. Their heart and soul would also experience the healing. He touched them in such a way that their lack of faith was also healed. Basically exclaiming through the healing that *"I am real, I am the Messiah and I have come to make you whole again, not just in your body from disease and decay, but in your faith. Not just in the exorcism of demons but also in your soul and in your mind. You have been set free from your captivity…now go and sin no more."*

"On the other side of the lake the crowds welcomed Jesus, because they had been waiting for him. Then a man named Jairus, a leader of the local synagogue, came and fell at Jesus's feet, pleading with him to come home with him. His only daughter, who was about 12 years old, was dying.

"As Jesus went with him, he was surrounded by the crowds." (Luke 8:40–42)

Ponder that for a moment. Jesus's fame had grown so much that he basically became a superstar and he was mobbed and surrounded by people everywhere he went. He was in such high demand that people would be waiting at the edge of the lake for him, welcoming him and hoping that they could just see him, listen to him preach the Good News and maybe even get a chance to touch him or be healed, and to receive some sense of hope in their captivity and disparity.

No wonder he chose a group as large as twelve to be his disciples and be by his side throughout his ministry. He needed a group of men to help him get through the crowds so as to not get smothered or completely overwhelmed by the people wanting him and longing for him, pushing and shoving to get to him so they could touch him and be healed.

In the middle of this story about Jairus and his 12 year old daughter dying, Jesus is on his way to his house to heal her when something unexpected happens within the enormous crowd that is following Jesus as they are traveling with him.

"A woman in the crowd had suffered for twelve years with constant bleeding. She had suffered a great deal from many doctors, and over the years she had spent everything she had to pay them, but she had gotten no better. In fact, she had gotten worse. She had heard about Jesus, so she came up behind him through the crowd and touched his robe. For she thought to herself, 'If I can just touch his robe, I will be healed.' Immediately the bleeding stopped, and she could feel in her body that she had been healed of her terrible condition.

"Jesus realized at once that healing power had gone out from him, so he turned around in the crowd and asked, 'Who touched my robe?'

"His disciples said to him, 'Look at this crowd pressing around you. How can you ask, 'Who touched me?'

"But he kept on looking around to see who had done it. Then the frightened woman, trembling at the realization of what had happened to her, came and fell to her knees in front of him and told him what she had done. And he said to her, 'Daughter, your faith has made you well. Go in peace. Your suffering is over.'" (Jesus, Gospel of Mark 5:25–34)

This is the healing I wanted to talk about for a moment.

"Your suffering is over."

There are not many in this world who can relate to the suffering this woman had to endure for twelve long and excruciating years of constant bleeding. I have deep sympathy for her pain, her discomfort, and her inability to find someone who can help her to stop the bleeding. My heart just breaks for her in her distress.

What I love reading, though, is her willingness and determination, her faith to pursue Jesus even amongst a crazy crowd to *"just touch his robe, and I will be healed."* Her courage and determination to fight through the crowd, probably weak from her plight, to seek out, find and then touch him. Her faith is extraordinary and I can only imagine that she was truly at the end of her rope. She had exhausted all possibilities of finding healing and became poor in the process. What an incredible story of faith, healing, courage and compassion.

It is remarkable to read how Jesus knew instantly that healing power had gone out from him to heal another faithful person needing to be made whole again. The circumstances around this healing explains more clearly just how much the act of her faith was, and is, a necessary part of the healing process.

"Daughter," he said to her, "*your faith* has made you well. Go in peace. Your suffering is over." (Jesus, Luke 8:48, emphasis mine)

Can you imagine her delight, her excitement, her heart exploding with the feelings and the truth of her predicament no longer being a part of her life after so many years of suffering? All of that is over now…Go in peace. Wow!

The other part of this story that I find fascinating is that this woman, who is still reeling from the transformation of her healing, would be trembling and frightened at the realization of what has just happened to her. She also realized that Jesus knows what she has done, like it is a bad thing for her to have taken the healing power from him without asking him first. It almost reads like she feels ashamed at her selfish motive to be healed and that Jesus is somehow going to punish her for her actions. Falling to her knees in front of him, trembling, confessing to Jesus what she had done and probably apologizing, asking for forgiveness.

But this is not your ordinary King. With her willingness and one last hope of healing, this woman, in her desperation, reached out with her hand in a crowd of many people all trying to get close to him to just touch the fringe of his robe. Hoping that he wouldn't even know that it was she who touched him. Man, I love that story.

Let's continue on with the rest of the story that we started with in the healing of Jairus's daughter.

"While he was still speaking to her, a messenger arrived from the home of Jairus, the leader of the synagogue. He told him, 'Your daughter is dead. There is no use troubling the Teacher now.'

"But when Jesus heard what had happened, he said to Jairus, 'Don't be afraid. Just have faith, and she will be healed.'

"When they arrived at the house, Jesus wouldn't let anyone go in with him except Peter, John, James and the little girl's father and mother. The house was filled with people weeping and wailing, but he said, 'Stop the weeping! She isn't dead; she's only asleep.'

"But the crowd laughed at him because they all knew she had died. Then Jesus took her by the hand and said in a loud voice, 'My child, get up!' And at that moment her life returned, and she immediately stood up! Then Jesus told them to give her something to eat. Her parents were overwhelmed, but Jesus insisted that they not tell anyone what had happened." (Luke 8:49–56)

As a parent, I can picture the euphoria of utter excitement, the massive flow of emotions that would follow such an immaculate miracle as this in the healing of this daughter who was already dead. Amazing!

I have one more miraculous healing that needs to be discussed. There are just so many amazing and beautiful stories that need to be retold. In John chapter 9, Jesus is taking advantage of a prime opportunity to teach his disciples and his followers another important lesson through this healing.

"As Jesus was walking along, he saw a man who had been blind from birth. 'Rabbi,' his disciples asked him 'why was this man born blind? Was it because of his own sins or his parents' sins?'

"'It was not because of his sins or his parents' sins,' Jesus answered. 'This happened so the power of God could be seen in him. We must quickly carry out the tasks assigned to us by the one who sent us. "'The night is coming, and then no one can work. But while I am here in the world, I am the light of the world.'

"Then he spit on the ground, made mud with the saliva, and spread the mud over the blind man's eyes. He told him, 'Go wash yourself in the pool of Siloam.' So the man went and washed and came back seeing.

"His neighbors and others who knew him as a blind beggar asked each other, 'Isn't this the man who used to sit and beg?' Some said he was, and others said, 'No, he just looks like him.'

"But the beggar kept saying, 'Yes, I am the same one!'

"They asked, 'Who healed you? What happened?'

"He told them, 'The man they call Jesus made mud and spread it over my eyes and told me, 'Go to the pool of Siloam and wash yourself.' So I went and washed, and now I can see!'

"'Where is he now?' they asked.

"'I don't know,' he replied.

"Then they took the man who had been blind to the Pharisees, because it was on the Sabbath that Jesus had made the mud and healed him. The Pharisees asked the man all about it. So he told them, 'He put the mud over my eyes, and when I washed it, I could see!'

"Some of the Pharisees said, 'This man Jesus is not from God, for he is working on the Sabbath.' Others said, 'But how could an ordinary sinner do such miraculous signs?' So there was a deep division of opinion among them." (John 9:1–16)

It simply amazes me every time I read how the Pharisees focus solely on the fact that Jesus healed on the Sabbath and not on the fact that "HE HEALED" someone. They are only concerned about what they believed he did wrong and not what the power of God had passionately done through him in his acts of love and compassion.

Jesus did not shy away from taking every opportunity to perform miracles, even at the most opportune times. He almost cherished opportunities to irritate the Pharisees in their legalistic religion, exploiting their unrealistic strict rules and regulations in choosing to act in love through the transformation of a physical deformity. Jesus knew full well what his actions and words would do to them. Setting a fire, the thirst for blood in the anger and fury that burst inside the Pharisees hardened hearts for what they considered blasphemy.

"Then the Pharisees again questioned the man who had been blind and demanded, 'What's your opinion about this man who healed you?'

"The man replied, 'I think he must be a prophet.'

"The Jewish leaders still refused to believe the man had been blind and could now see, so they called in his parents. They asked them, 'Is this your son? Was he born blind? If so, how can he now see?'

"His parents replied, 'We know this is our son and that he was born blind, but we do not know how he can see or who healed him. Ask him. He is old enough to speak for himself.' His parents said this because they were afraid of the Jewish leaders, who had announced that anyone saying Jesus was the Messiah would be expelled from the synagogue. That's why they said, 'He is old enough. Ask him.'

"So for the second time they called in the man who had been blind and told him, 'God should get the glory for this, because we know this man Jesus is a sinner.'

"'I don't know whether he is a sinner,' the man replied. 'But I know this: I was blind, and now I can see!'

"But what did he do?' they asked. 'How did he heal you?'

"'Look!' the man exclaimed. 'I told you once. Didn't you listen? Why do you want to hear it again? Do you want to become his disciples, too?'

"Then they cursed him and said, 'You are his disciple, but we are disciples of Moses! We know God spoke to Moses, but we don't even know where this man comes from.'

"'Why, that's very strange!' the man replied. 'He healed my eyes, and yet you don't know where he comes from? We know that God doesn't listen to sinners, but he is ready to hear those who worship him and do his will. Ever since the world began, no one has been able to open the eyes of someone born blind. If this man were not from God, he couldn't have done it.'

"'You were born a total sinner!' they answered. 'Are you trying to teach us?' And they threw him out of the synagogue." (John 9:17–34)

Pride and religious legalism that people portray causes those who say "they can see" to be completely blind to the absolute love and truth of Jesus Christ. It is still happening today in many different "religions," churches, and various other belief systems throughout our world.

"When Jesus heard what had happened, he found the man and asked, 'Do you believe in the Son of Man?'

"The man answered, 'Who is he, sir? I want to believe in him.'

"'You have seen him,' Jesus said, 'and he is speaking to you.'

"'Yes, Lord, I believe!' the man said. And he worshipped Jesus.

"Then Jesus told him, 'I entered this world to render judgment—to give sight to the blind and to show those who think they can see that they are blind.'

"Some Pharisees who were standing nearby heard him and asked, 'Are you saying we're blind?'

"'If you were blind, you wouldn't be guilty,' Jesus replied. 'But you remain guilty because you claim you can see.'" (John 9:35–41)

This whole passage is filled to the brim with so many fascinating messages. Wow, what an extraordinary story. Let's start first with how important it is to know that Jesus is the light of the world. I just absolutely love knowing this. Every ounce of light that you see, every act of love, every act of kindness or forgiveness…is wrapped up in Jesus. Pure light shining over and throughout our lives.

One of the things that is so interesting is how he can just touch a leper and he is made whole and clean again. But with this blind man, he has to take a whole different approach to healing him. Spitting on the ground, mixing his saliva with the dirt, he makes mud which is then applied to the man's eyes. So interesting. But what I love about this story is the dialogue that takes place between the blind man and the Pharisees.

A simple man, blind since birth, uneducated and poor, is able to understand perfectly well what has taken place within the miracle that has happened to himself in the power of Jesus. And yet, these highly educated, highly profiled religious leaders who think so loftily of themselves cannot get past their own ignorance and blindness because of their legalistic religion, to see something so pure and beautiful in this man Jesus. The miracle that has taken place makes claim that he is the Christ, the Messiah that they have been waiting for all these years.

What a perfect example that is being displayed for all of us to see that so easily reflects our own legalism clearly present even now today.

Be very careful that you yourselves do not fall into the trap of religious legalism. Jesus made his command and desire of us very clear.

"You must love the Lord your God with all your heart, all your soul and all your mind. This is the first and greatest commandment. A second is equally important: Love your neighbor as yourself." (Jesus, Gospel of Matthew 22:37–39)

With all the sin and ugliness that each of us carry, none of us is perfect, therefore you are not perfect and neither is your neighbor. If we are to love our neighbor as we love ourselves, I believe then we must love everyone the same. No one is without sin, not the person sitting beside you, working beside you, going to school with you or who happens to live next door to you. In fact, you may need to start by learning to love yourself first!

Religious legalism is a trap for those who feel like they know better than the next person, or that they are more religious, have less sin or are more favored in the eyes of God. You may think you have it all dialed in or that you are more "righteous" or "religious" than your neighbor. Wrong! Get over yourself. We are all equally loved in the eyes of God. You are only hurting and hindering those who are searching for God with your legalism. Love each other is what we are supposed to do…commanded to do.

Love everyone…do not judge, do not be prideful or to the point of thinking you are more worthy, more valued than your neighbor, or more loved because you have chosen a different path. God loves us all and we also should love others, and that means everyone.

Blind guides leading the blind. Thank you, Jesus, for loving us so much as to show us the way. Teaching us in every way through your Word all that is so clearly right in front of us.

At the beginning of this chapter, I really had no idea what direction this was going to go. In fact, that is the way this whole book has been. I have had the initial idea of each chapter but had no idea where it would end up or where God would take me. I hope you are enjoying this as much as I am, for I am being led by the Holy Spirit to write down these words in this book for all to read, contemplate, process and hopefully shine light into your life, your heart, and your soul.

The healings of Jesus are just one part of many parts surrounding this hero to so many people. His words, his life, his example and his touch bring to the world something unreal and unexplainable to the point of asking "Who is this man?" Who is this man that chose to purposefully allow himself to be flogged with thirty-nine lashes? Who is this man who allowed soldiers to mock him, spit on him, nail him to a wooden beam and then hang him up on a tree?

Here we have this man, the Son of God, the Messiah, who only showed love and compassion to everyone, being beaten and nailed to the edge of his life and he *Still* would not hold any anger, no retaliation, and no grudge…only love…

"Father forgive them for they do not know what they are doing." (Luke 23:34)

This is the man I want to follow. This is the God I want to believe in. Jesus the Christ showed us all without any reserve the true essence of his title through his healings. He revealed to us the love that enveloped him, the compassion that surrounded him, and finally, the one true purpose which he came down to this earth he created. He was born a baby, lived as a man, served as our healer, taught as our Teacher, loved us as our friend and died and rose again, defeating death once and for all as our Savior and King. He came for us, everyone one of us, to save us and bring us home. No one is exempt from his love!

"I have told you these things, so that in me you may have peace. In this world you will have trouble. But take heart! I have overcome the world." (Jesus, John 16:33)

"For I have come down from heaven to do the will of God who sent me, not to do my own will. And this is the will of God, that I should not lose even one of all those he has given me, but that I should raise them up at the last day. For it is my Father's will that all who see his Son and believe in him should have eternal life. I will raise them up at the last day." (Jesus, Gospel of John 6:38–40)

Chapter 8

Miraculous

"It is not the task of Christianity to provide easy answers to every question, but to make us progressively aware of a mystery. God is not so much the object of our knowledge as the cause of our wonder."
—Kallistos Ware

"Faith is the confidence that what we hope
for will actually happen, it gives us assurance
about things we cannot see."

—Hebrews 11:1

*"Miracles happen every day, change your perception of
what a miracle is and you'll see them all around you."*
—Jon Bon Jovi

*"Miracles are a retelling in small letters of the very
same story which is written across the whole world
in letters too large for some of us to see."*
—C. S. Lewis

"Then Jesus told them, 'A prophet is honored everywhere except in his hometown and among his relatives and his own family.' And because of their unbelief, he couldn't do any miracles among them except to place his hands on a few sick people and heal them. And he was amazed at their unbelief." (Mark 6:4–6)

According to *Merriam-Webster* the definition of a *miracle* is "an extraordinary event manifesting divine intervention in human affairs."

I already touched base on a few of Jesus's miracles through his healings in the last chapter, but in this chapter I would like to discuss the mind-bending miracles outside the realm of his healings.

Because Jesus was God in the flesh, he was given the power to do his will either in his healings or through his miracles whenever he felt it was necessary or when he was trying to point out the obvious in his clear message that he is who he says *He* is…the Messiah who is bringing Good News to all who will believe in him. He also said many times that he was only doing what the Father wanted him to do and that he and the Father were one and the same.

As you can see in the verses from the Gospel of Mark quoted above, faith has to be a component for these miracles and healings to take place. But there are also certain miracles that Jesus performed just for the sake of the people "so that you would believe."

As I begin to investigate the deep ripple effect of his miracles and the extensive faith that is wrapped up in them, I have to be realistic in the skepticism of those who have a hard time believing any of it ever existed, including the healings of Jesus. The only proof of these miracles, either in the here and now or even from the time of Jesus is based solely on faith. But that faith first starts in the core of believing that Jesus is who he says he is: The true Son of God and the creator of all that is around us.

Miracles, by most people's definition, fall somewhere between the miracles of Christ and something that has happened in their own life, or to someone they know. I believe miracles happen every day and it only takes a moment to step out of our everyday life and our routine to notice the miracles that are in plain sight everywhere around us. If you have children, then you have already experienced one of the greatest miracles in the example of childbirth.

Miracles can be defined in the simplistic beauty of nature that is all around us. It can be defined in the scientific and mathematical equations of how the earth, the sun and the moon all work together to help sustain life on this planet so we, as humans can survive. To breathe air, find food that is naturally grown for us to eat and survive is a miracle. The food that is in our oceans, lakes, and rivers has sustained life since the beginning of time. The amazing process in which our bodies function with its thousands of different parts all working together to help us live, thrive and grow is simply a miracle.

Let me make something absolutely clear.

To even believe a miracle can happen must involve the faith of the recipient, and or friends and family who are either praying for it to happen, or expects it to happen. When Jesus said... "*Your faith has made you well.*"...he was clearly stating that because the recipient of the miraculous healing believed he was the Son of God and was confident he WOULD heal them, only then were they able to be healed. They believed; therefore, it happened.

Now, let's make sure that we also point out that some miracles don't happen and that is certainly not because of the person's lack of faith. It is, for a reason we are unaware of, that God has a different plan, another purpose. His will is not our will...and that is why He is

God and we are not. And because we are the clay and he is the potter, we have to trust that his will is better. This is still one of the most difficult barriers to those who accept Christ and those who don't.

I had a really good friend years ago (we are still friends but live far apart) who basically shot down any chance of believing in God because his prayers to heal his mom seemed, to him, to go unheard. His mom was his rock and only source of real love. When God did not answer his prayers to heal his mom…well then, he was done. He chose from this outcome that there was no need to convince him otherwise. His answer came in the results of his unanswered prayers. I would venture to say that there are many who have lived a similar tale as this one.

In fact, many choose to not believe in God or believe that Jesus is the Son of God, simply because of that which they *can* see. All the turmoil and death from so many different trials in the world such as war, natural disasters, disease, etc., distort the views of those who want to know why a loving God who is all powerful does not stop these things from happening. Where is God in all of this?

I will never forget while trying to have this discussion with this friend of mine as to why I believe in Jesus. He straight up asked me, "Then why didn't he heal my mom when I prayed and asked for her to be healed?" I didn't have an answer.

It is a never ending circular struggle to convince the mind from the heart that God knows what he is doing. I can only say that in my life, my own little, measly life, I have seen the hands of God at work in many different lives through many different people choosing to believe that God is still working and performing miracles all the time and through many who call out his name.

I believe prayer is just as powerful now as it was two thousand years ago. But it has to begin somewhere. What will start the process of faith? When do we get out of our own way, silence our ignorance and bullheadedness, and just simply believe and have a child-like faith of all that is before our eyes?

As I sit here, contemplating all that is in our existence, I can observe fairly clearly that this life, in and of itself, is a miracle—plain and simple. All of it. Our planet, our lives, the air we breathe, the creatures that walk this earth and swim in our bodies of water. The discoveries from science, our DNA, our space and stars, our time, birth and death…all are simply a miracle…happening over and over again right before our very eyes!

Because of the continuous flow of regeneration and season after season, we begin to just expect there to be flowers blooming in the spring, baby animals born and our population continuing to grow. Death and life are just a part of the process. We don't blink an eye to the simple, but miraculous act of nature that just automatically takes its course. But we certainly don't have all the answers to the mysteries that continue to rattle our brains. We, as humans, have been searching and discovering how this thing called life really works. And year after year, we learn more of the mysteries of this life and God pulls back the curtain a tad bit more.

For those that truly call themselves Christians, we already know and believe in life after death, eternal life, and have the answers to the questions that once haunted us. Because of our faith, we know where our final destination is. We know what we believe. I am writing this book for those who are struggling to believe. For those whose faith is weak or possibly nonexistent. I am hoping to reach the lost, the hurt, the broken and the sick. To reach those that are searching for truth… searching for answers. Searching for Jesus.

How many stories have you heard when someone has only months to live because of a huge inoperable tumor that is on their brain? Then, a week later, they go in to get an x-ray and the tumor is completely gone. With no answer in sight and the doctors haven't a clue, the only logical answer is that God chose to perform a miracle for his purpose. It was a miracle that was answered through prayer. Your faith is only limited by what you choose to believe is possible. If we all had faith like a child, there would be a heck of a lot more miracles happening around us.

I have come to the understanding through my faith that God knows *far* better than I do how this life will be played out. I have already come to the conclusion that in life bad things happen. They just do. It is not God's fault, and it is not always our fault. Sometimes it is our fault resulting from a poor choice and sometimes it isn't. If we choose to separate ourselves from him, then we are choosing to not invest in our relationship with him. If his hand is removed and our faith is diminished…then he can't do much for us can he?

If we give up on our faith in Christ, then get mad at him for allowing something bad to happen, whose fault is that? Not God's fault. This does not mean, that since our faith is weak, we shall suffer more. Or that bad things will happen to us. It simply means that good things happen to bad people and bad things happen to good people, and vice versa. The rain will fall on the good and the bad.

If we accept the reality of our fate being that we all eventually die, one way or another, then the natural aspects of our lives, those who live long healthy lives and those who don't, are all a natural part of the process of life. It isn't fair by any means but it just is what it is. None of us know when our time here is done nor do we know the plans that God has for our lives. The best we can do is choose to make him our priority. Then His plan will eventually unfold within your life and your purpose will be revealed. And just to be sure… there may be many plans for your life that God has already made plans for…we just have to be willing and ready for his timing to put those plans in motion.

In my own life, there have been many times where I have prayed for God to do a miracle and for whatever reason, it didn't happen. And then there were times like the day I was praying for God to fix my car as I was driving it down the highway and for whatever reason my prayer was answered.

I was desperate for money and I was hoping to sell this old car I owned but as I drove it down the highway, speeding and slowing down, it was banging and making all sorts of crazy noises. This car was truly on its last legs but I really needed to sell it for the price I was asking for so I could make my mortgage payment. Not long after I prayed I exited the freeway and sure enough, it purred like a kitten. I kid you not!

Here I was, praying for something that really was not completely significant in the scheme of life, but yet, because I believed and asked for this in Jesus's name, he fixed it. Seriously, I don't have a mechanical bone in my whole body, and I know how this sounds, but that is exactly what happened.

I think it is important to explain that even though the car was running perfectly, there was a bit of time there where I thought at any moment this car could and would go right back to the way it was just a few minutes ago. But thankfully I can tell you that it didn't. And when the guys came to test drive the car it started right up, still purring like it was on the freeway. They eventually drove away with it and I thanked God for that gift.

I cried while driving that car that day knowing full well and for whatever reason, God decided to bless me and answer my prayer. I know that there will be those people out there that will try and justify as to why this particular car decided to fix itself and that's fine. I know what happened and I will always believe that God answered my desperate prayer that day.

I have another story that I would like to share with you that not too many people even know about. It was a miracle that I will never forget.

Back in 2013, when God had called me personally to put together the Save the Children Yard sale, my goal was to raise $15,000, which would then be given to a charitable nonprofit organization called *Planet Changer*. This organization would then build wells in Uganda for clean drinking water so kids would no longer be getting sick or dying from the contaminated and diseased water sources that were available to them. (And by the way, I just found out that I will be going back to Uganda this November, 2019, to see the wells and the people who have been blessed with clean water! Very exciting!)

After it was all said and done and after expenses were paid, God had blessed our endeavor and we ended up raising over $25,000 from that four day, gigantic community yard sale.

Over the course of that sale, every day, we would go around to the different paying stations and take a collection of money so as to not have too much available that would be tempting for someone to steal. Each drop that was taken was then counted and the amount was written on a piece of paper which was then wrapped up with a rubber band.

Over the course of four days and at the end of the sale, as you can probably imagine, we had many rolls of cash and checks that were intertwined that had been gathered up and counted. What took place next would have to fall under the category of miraculous.

After the yard sale was over and all cleaned up, my mom and I were sitting at the dining room table. I took out the calculator and started adding up the rolls of cash and checks by the number that was written on the piece of paper attached to the outside of each roll. After all was counted and the expenses taken out, the total ended up around $20,000.

Now $20,000 is an amazing accomplishment considering it is a yard sale but what happened next, I just can't explain.

After I counted the rolls, I needed to then separate everything so I could organize it and get it ready to take it to the bank and transfer it into cashier's checks made out to *Planet Changer* and *World Vision*. *World Vision* is another organization that I wanted to sponsor for their amazing work in meeting the needs of children all over the world. After I separated the checks and the cash, I went ahead and counted the cash, twice. Each time coming up with the same number. The total combination of checks and cash came out to just over $20,000. And like I said earlier, this was after the expenses were paid. I remember feeling a bit bummed hoping that it was a bit more but still so grateful for the blessings that God had given us through this sale.

After I got to the bank and handed them all the cash, the bank then proceeded to put the money through their extremely fast cash counter. You know the one that makes all those flipping sounds as it is counting the cash super-fast? They then informed me that my numbers were off on the amount I had given them according to what I had counted at my house.

Now, you have to understand. I counted that money twice and I know what I counted.

The people at the bank, after it was counted, told me that there was just over $5,000 more in the amount of cash from the amount that I had originally told them it was. I asked them, "Are you sure?" So I had them count the money again, and once again it was the greater amount. I was in complete shock. I asked for the money back, went home with my heart pounding and goose bumps everywhere and counted it again. And in that moment, as I sat down again to count the money, sure enough, there was over $5,000 more and not the amount I had originally counted…twice. My mom, whose faith is strong, just sat there smiling at me with a big grin, knowing full well that God had just multiplied the amount of cash I had originally counted.

As you can probably guess, my heart was overflowing with love and the tears started streaming down my face…God had struck again with his amazing love and compassion.

I was called upon to fulfill a mission that God has chosen me to complete. In my obedience to this calling, he blessed me tenfold. He gave me purpose and meaning and I finally felt like I was making a difference in the lives of children, storing up treasures in heaven. Then, God chose to step right in the middle of it all and perform this miracle that blew my mind and heart wide open.

Trust me when I say this, God loves his children and wants to love you in every way. He has shown me in so many different ways that he is alive and present in my life and has every desire to meet the needs of his children.

Over the course of those four days, there just isn't any chance that the money that was rolled and counted and then counted by me twice, in front of my mom, could have been off by that much money.

That, my friends, was simply a miracle. There really is no other way that could have happened. I could see a $100 or even $2–300 but $5,000? Nope. That was a gift from God only adding to the miracle of raising that much money in a yard sale for the benefit of his children who needed it so much more than I. That was an answer to prayer…and God followed through, because of faith.

When we step out into the unknown and have faith in a God who can do anything…everything can happen. I saw miracle after miracle throughout that yard sale and the following one I did three years later. God moves and magnifies. He is the God of miracles, which I have absolutely no doubt about.

It is not only fascinating, but completely intriguing what the Gospels bring to the life of Jesus regarding his miracles. He turned water into wine, fed the five thousand and then fed four thousand more. He walked on water and commanded the wind, the storm and the waves to hush.

But let us not forget, that the immaculate conception of Jesus was the first miracle.

"In the sixth month of Elizabeth's pregnancy, God sent the angel Gabriel to Nazareth, a village in Galilee, to a virgin named Mary. She was engaged to be married to a man named Joseph, a descendant of King David. Gabriel appeared to her and said, 'Greetings, favored woman! The Lord is with you.'

"Confused and disturbed, Mary tried to think what the angel could mean. 'Don't be afraid, Mary,' the angel told her, 'for you have found favor with God! You will conceive and give birth to a son, and you will name him Jesus. He will be very great and will be called the Son of the Most High. The Lord God will give him the throne of his ancestor David. And he will reign over Israel forever; his Kingdom will never end!'

"Mary asked the angel, 'But how can this happen? I am a virgin.'

"The angel replied, 'The Holy Spirit will come upon you, and the power of the Most High will overshadow you. So the baby to be born will be holy, and he will be called the Son of God. For nothing is impossible with God.'

"Mary responded, 'I am the Lord's servant. May everything you have said about me come true.' And then the angel left her." (Luke 1:26–35, 38)

To be surprised by Jesus's miracles, or to even be skeptical of them, is to question the whole story of the Bible. Everyone has doubts and barriers to their belief system, and that is okay. God designed us to think, observe, process and question. He wants our faith to come from our own choice. I believe and have faith simply because of my relationship with Christ. No one who is alive and breathing on this planet right now has any proof or is a witness to any of the miracles of the Bible or that they actually happened. You either choose to believe them or you don't. We have many eye witness testimonies that date within fifty years of the events which took place over two thousand years ago, but that is still based on the faith that these events ever really occurred.

Why do millions or even billions believe in the story of Christmas? Because quite honestly, we want to and we need to. So we can believe in the hope of mankind. So we can believe in the validity of love…in forgiveness…in kindness and of giving. That there is a God who loves us so much as to give us an opportunity for a second chance to this life in the Way of His Son and a way out of our misery. To give us hope in something more than what we have now or ever will. Our world, our people, desperately need something to believe in outside of themselves. We are hoping and praying to see change happen in the people around us so that humanity can shed the ugly blemishes of our history and truth. So that, so much of the darkness, fear and pain can be wiped out.

We need to believe that there is more than what this world has to offer. There is more than just working until we die, paying taxes and retiring on too little to survive. There is more to growing old, getting sick and then simply dying, never to be remembered again. There has to be more than just collecting stuff and then more stuff, always trying to fill that void with everything but the love and forgiveness of God.

Jesus performed many miracles that are recorded in the New Testament and often get overlooked either because of the message that is being conveyed or simply because it is not as miraculous as raising someone from the dead.

Jesus's miracles range from cursing a fig tree to wither up and die because it never produced fruit, to when he told Peter to go fishing for a silver coin that will be found in the mouth of the first fish he catches so they can pay the temple tax. But his greatest and most profound miracle, other than his own Resurrection, has to be the raising of Lazarus.

But first, let us not forget about walking on water, which is a miracle that would have been so incredible to have been a witness to. But like the disciples, I would have freaked out also, seeing someone walking toward me while I sat in a boat in the middle of crashing waves and darkness.

The raising of Lazarus was something on a whole different level. This man had been dead for four days lying in a tomb. ***Four days!*** And trust me, the stench in the air from this dying man could not have been very good either.

Listen to this miraculous story in the eleventh chapter of John.

"A man named Lazarus was sick. He lived in Bethany with his sisters, Mary and Martha. This is the Mary who later poured the expensive perfume on the Lord's feet and wiped them with her hair. Her brother, Lazarus, was sick. So the two sisters sent a message to Jesus telling him, 'Lord, your dear friend is very sick.'

"But when Jesus heard about it he said, 'Lazarus's sickness will not end in death. No, it happened for the glory of God so that the Son of God will receive glory from this.' So although Jesus loved Martha, Mary, and Lazarus, he stayed where he was for the next two days. Finally, he said to his disciples, 'Let's go back to Judea.'

"But his disciples objected. 'Rabbi,' they said, 'only a few days ago the people in Judea were trying to stone you. Are you going there again?'

"Jesus replied, 'There are twelve hours of daylight every day. During the day people can walk safely. They can see because they have the light of this world. But at night there is danger of stumbling because they have no light.' Then he said, 'Our friend Lazarus has fallen asleep, but now I will go and wake him up.'

"The disciples said, 'Lord, if he is sleeping, he will soon get better!' They thought Jesus meant Lazarus was simply sleeping, but Jesus meant Lazarus had died.

"So he told them plainly, 'Lazarus is dead. And for your sakes, I'm glad I wasn't there, for now you will really believe. Come, let's go see him.'

"When Jesus arrived at Bethany, he was told that Lazarus had already been in his grave for four days. Bethany was only a few miles down the road from Jerusalem, and many of the people had come to console Martha and Mary in their loss. When Martha got word that Jesus was coming, she went to meet him. But Mary stayed in the house. Martha said to Jesus, 'Lord, if only you had been here, my brother would not have died. But even now I know that God will give you whatever you ask.'

"Jesus told her, 'Your brother will rise again.'

"'Yes,' Martha said, 'he will rise when everyone else rises, at the last day.'

"Jesus told her, '*I am the resurrection and the life. Anyone who believes in me will live, even after dying. Everyone who lives in me and believes in me will never ever die.* Do you believe this, Martha?'

"'Yes, Lord,' she told him. 'I have always believed you are the Messiah, the Son of God, the one who has come into the world from God.' Then she returned to Mary. She called Mary aside from the mourners and told her, 'The Teacher is here and wants to see you.' So Mary immediately went to him.

"Jesus had stayed outside the village, at the place where Martha met him. When the people who were at the house consoling Mary saw her leave so hastily, they assumed she was going to Lazarus's grave to weep. So they followed her there. When Mary arrived and saw Jesus, she fell at his feet and said, 'Lord, if you only had been here, my brother would not have died.'

"When Jesus saw her weeping and saw the other people wailing with her, a deep anger welled up within him, and he was deeply troubled. 'Where have you put him?' he asked them.

"They told him, 'Lord, come and see.' Then Jesus wept. The people who were standing nearby said, 'See how much he loved him!' But some said, 'This man healed a blind man. Couldn't he have kept Lazarus from dying?'

"Jesus was still angry as he arrived at the tomb, a cave with a stone rolled across its entrance. 'Roll the stone aside,' Jesus told them.

"But Martha, the dead man's sister, protested, 'Lord, he has been dead for four days. The smell will be terrible.'

"Jesus responded, 'Didn't I tell you that you would see God's glory if you believe?' So they rolled the stone aside. Then Jesus looked up to heaven and said, 'Father, thank you for hearing me. You always hear me, but I said it loud for the sake of all these people standing here, so that they will believe you sent me.' Then Jesus shouted, 'Lazarus, come out!'

"And the dead man came out, his hands and feet bound in grave-clothes, his face wrapped in a head cloth. Jesus told them, 'Unwrap him and let him go!'

"Many of the people who were with Mary believed in Jesus when they saw this happen. But some went to the Pharisees and told them what Jesus had done. Then the leading priests and Pharisees called the high council together. 'What are we going to do?' they asked each other. 'This man certainly performs many miraculous signs. If we allow him to go on like this, soon everyone will believe in him. Then the Roman army will come and destroy both our Temple and our nation.'

"Caiaphas, who was high priest at that time, said, 'You don't know what you are talking about! You don't realize that it's better for you that one man should die for the people than for the whole nation to be destroyed.'

"He did not say this on his own; as high priest at that time he was led to prophesy that Jesus would die for the entire nation. And not only for that nation, but to bring together and unite all the children of God scattered around the world.

"So from that point on, the Jewish leaders began to plot Jesus' death." (John 11:1-53)

This miracle is easily one of my favorites. I would have given anything to have had the chance to see this take place right before my very eyes.

I have to believe just one of Jesus's miracles would have been enough for me to drop everything to follow him.

This miracle of Jesus, surprisingly, is only found in the Gospel of John. For me though, it does not make it any less true or that there is a greater chance this miracle did not take place. I believe that John found it so profound that he made sure to testify about it and to go so far as to give us so much detail around it that it almost filled an entire chapter. This was the pinnacle of Jesus's miracles and the apostle John made sure to capture its complete essence.

I highly recommend the movie, *Jesus of Nazareth*. It is still my favorite movie, so far, that exemplifies the life and ministry of Jesus Christ. This story of Lazarus rising from the dead is in this movie and it is simply amazing. I get goosebumps every time I watch this scene unfold in front of my eyes. Jesus is standing in front of the open tomb praying to the Father, tears streaming down his face, thanking him for this opportunity to reveal his glory to all the people standing everywhere, watching and waiting to see another mind-bending miracle. Then, Jesus raises him arms in the air and shouts out loudly with absolute authority… "Lazarus, come out!"

So incredibly powerful and moving. I love seeing this visual come to life showing us clearly that Jesus has extreme authority over the powers of death and decay. This is Good News indeed!

I would like to point out some of the highlights of this passage of Scripture, as I feel there needs to be some added discussion around the contents.

Jesus knows all too well that this event is his last chance before his final masterpiece, the Resurrection, to move people in the direction of belief and to have faith that he is truly the Messiah, the Son of God.

"And for your sakes, I'm glad I wasn't there, for now you will really believe." (John 11:15)

What is amazing about this statement is that he says this to his disciples and I am assuming, his followers. Almost implying that they have yet to go all in to believe and be sold out for Jesus. Which baffles me because, how much proof do you need? Aren't all the miracles he has done so far enough? The miracle of walking on water wasn't enough? Fascinating.

I love how Jesus quotes and prophesies about himself way before it is going to happen. When Jesus says to Martha, *"I am the resurrection and the life. Anyone who believes in me will live, even after dying."*

How incredibly consoling is that truth!? I don't know about you… but that, right there, is the icing on the cake. First, he prophesies his resurrection from the dead and then completes it by letting everyone else know, that anyone who believes in him shall **also do the same**! Best news ever!

One of things about Jesus that is only mentioned a few times is when Jesus gets angry. This, for me, is also consoling because it just goes to show that Jesus was also human, his compassion for his friends and the anger that death has stolen from them, I believe, irritates Jesus to no end. In fact, he was angry all the way to the grave site.

"And then Jesus wept." (John 11:35)

One of the many things I love to read about in the Gospels is the loving relationship that Jesus has with our Father in heaven.

"Father, thank you for hearing me. You always hear me, but I said it out loud for the sake of all these people standing here, so that they will believe you sent me." (Jesus, Gospel of John 11:41)

Lazarus didn't come out of the grave unwrapped and clean without the smell of death on him. He came out as someone who surely was dead and is now alive again through the powerful miracle and example of Jesus Christ in all of God's glory. And who did Jesus give the glory to? He gave the glory to God. In fact, Lazarus still had on his head, the head cloth, and his hands and feet still bound by the grave clothes. It is amazing that he was even able to walk out of that tomb.

Can you picture this scene? Jesus tells them to roll away the huge stone lying in front of the cave. If Lazarus is able to walk out of this cave, it must have been a pretty good size cave. Then, Jesus, with a loud voice yells out… "*Lazarus, Come Out!*" Then, after a few seconds, which probably felt like forever, Lazarus walks out of the shadows of the darkness from that cave and into the direct sunlight. This man, who is no longer trapped by the clutches of death, is alive again after lying in this tomb for four days! Jaw-dropping to be sure.

To the overwhelming and complete shock of all the people standing there, watching and witnessing such a miracle, this had to have been the greatest testament to the proof of Jesus's claims as the true Messiah. Martha and Mary, the sisters of Lazarus, must have been ecstatic and filled with such an overwhelming joy, crying, and weeping at the feet of Jesus in complete love and praise! For their Savior had once again answered their prayers. Wow…if only to have been there!

After seeing something like this, and if my faith in Jesus was wavering or if there was any doubt left, this would have put me over the edge.

This is the stuff I love to read and ponder. This is also, in my mind, a glimpse into the near future of the events that will soon take place. This man, who just rose Lazarus from the dead, would himself, follow suit to the example laid out for everyone to see. His death and most memorable miracle, the Resurrection, was just around the corner.

Lastly, it amazes me, to the depths of complete ignorance that these Pharisees and religious leaders had at this time in choosing to not see so clearly who this man, the Son of God, truly was. How blind they must have been by their own hardened hearts. They were so consumed by their ego, ignorance, greed and selfish motives, that they couldn't even open their eyes to see or their hearts to believe, that this man was truly the Christ. Even after he raises a man to life after being dead for four days, this is still not strong enough proof for them? Simply amazing.

To me, it seems like they are far more concerned with losing their stature, their earthly significance, and false royalty as religious and pompous leaders, than they were to open their hearts and minds and believe that this truly was and is the Messiah that they have been waiting for. Unbelievable is what they were and who they chose to be. Men, lacking in faith, and subdued by their own proclaimed magnificence.

In all reality, and at such a historical time as this, they served their purpose for who and what they were created to be. Somebody had to betray Jesus; somebody had to accuse him falsely, even to the point of death on a cross, so all of us could be saved. Jesus knew this would happen. He knew exactly what he was doing every time he angered the Pharisees by performing miracles of healing on the Sabbath which, according to them, was against the laws of Moses. But this was all a part of God's glorious plan. God wanted to redeem us, and to cleanse us with the blood of Jesus. To save us from ourselves. It was His pain and our gain.

"But despite all the miraculous signs Jesus had done, most of the people still did not believe in him. This is exactly what Isaiah the prophet had predicted:

"'Lord, who has believed our message? To whom has the Lord revealed his powerful arm?'" (Isaiah 53:1)

"But the people couldn't believe, for as Isaiah also said,

"'The Lord has blinded their eyes and hardened their hearts—so that their eyes cannot see, and their hearts cannot understand, and they cannot turn to me and have me heal them.'" (Isaiah 6:10)

"Isaiah was referring to Jesus when he said this, because he saw the future and spoke of the Messiah's glory. Many people did believe in him, however, including some of the Jewish leaders. But they wouldn't admit it for fear that the Pharisees would expel them from the synagogue. For they loved human praise more than the praise of God.

"Jesus shouted to the crowds, 'If you trust me, you are trusting not only me, but also God who sent me. For when you see me, you are seeing the one who sent me. I have come as a light to shine in this dark world, so that all who put their trust in me will no longer remain in the dark. I will not judge those who hear me but don't obey me, for I have come to save the world and not to judge it. But all who reject me and my message will be judged on the day of judgement by the truth I have spoken." (Jesus, John 12:37–48, emphasis mine)

Thank you, Jesus, for shedding your blood for us, alone and abandoned, suffering an intense flogging, beatings and falsely accused, you **chose** to take our place on that cross…and because of your stripes, because of your sacrifice, we are now healed and truly redeemed.

"But he was wounded for our transgressions, he was bruised for our iniquities; the chastisement for our peace was upon him, and by his stripes we are healed." (Isaiah 53:5)

I look forward to the day when I get to look into your eyes, thank you personally for all of your blessings and love, your forgiveness. I will finally be able to wrap my arms around you, place my tear stained cheek against yours and just embrace you. Enjoying the moment that I finally get to settle into your arms with a heart overflowing with love and a soul at total peace, with you, forever, into eternity...for that will truly be the best day ever.

I can only imagine...

"Don't worry about anything; instead, pray about everything. Tell God what you need, and thank him for all he has done. Then you will experience God's peace, which exceeds anything we can understand. His peace will guard your hearts and minds as you live in Christ Jesus." (Paul, Philippians 4:6–7)

Chapter 9

Truth and Light

"I am the way, the truth, and the life. No one can come to the Father except through me."
—Jesus, Gospel of John 14:6

"Jesus spoke to the people once more and said, 'I am the light of the world. If you follow me, you won't have to walk in darkness, because you will have the light that leads to life.'"

—Jesus, Gospel of John 8:12

"There is much more we would like to say about this, but it is difficult to explain, especially since you are spiritually dull and don't seem to listen. You have been believers so long now that you ought to be teaching others. Instead, you need someone to teach you again the basic things about God's word.

"You are like babies who need milk and cannot eat solid food. For someone who lives on milk is still an infant and doesn't know how to do what is right. Solid food is for those who are mature, who through training have the skill to recognize the difference between right and wrong."

—Hebrews 5:11–14

As I read and contemplate the words of Jesus, the Apostle Paul and all the other authors' letters and books of the New Testament, I am overwhelmed with joy by the simplistic but powerful messages within the explanations of who Jesus truly is and the direct correlation that these messages of love, hope, peace and forgiveness have with us… his creation.

Reading and studying the Word of God, if it is accepted with faith like a child, is a heart-transforming experience. The Scriptures are exceptionally historic in nature, geography and prophesy, and through many years of archaeology, God's Word becomes reality and has been found to be extraordinarily accurate. It becomes a bright light…illuminating its love, healing, and truth throughout your mind, your soul and your body. We become one with its heartbeat because the Word is alive and it is working and thriving to be used and grasped, written on your hearts.

"We proclaim to you the one who existed from the beginning, whom we have heard and seen. We saw him with our own eyes and touched him with our own hands. He is the Word of life. This one who is life itself was revealed to us, and we have seen him. And now we testify and proclaim to you that he is the one who is eternal life. He was with the Father, and then he was revealed to us. We proclaim to you what we ourselves have actually seen and heard so that you may have fellowship with us. And our fellowship is with the Father and with his Son, Jesus Christ. We are writing these things so that you may fully share our joy. This is the message we heard from Jesus and now declare to you: God is light, and there is no darkness in him at all." (1 John 1:1–5)

All of us desperately need this truth to survive and we should also be applying it to our lives so we can grow in our faith. This is the foundation to which we build our lives upon. This is where our faith is transformed, our hearts are filled overflowing with the love of Jesus and the fruit of our lives are then seen by everyone.

I believe without a doubt, that God wants us to dive deep into his Word, chew on it as long as you have to so that eventually you will develop a deep, heartfelt understanding of his love for us in the sacrifice of his beloved Son, Jesus.

As I have been writing this book, I have been diligently scanning my Bible, a New Living Translation Bible, looking for verses, stories, correlation, and corroboration, allowing the Holy Spirit to guide me in finding the Scriptures that will bring to life with eloquence and spiritual awakening the truths, love and grace that can be found within those pages. I can only hope that I have served this purpose well.

I hope you also have noticed and recognized just how much the Holy Spirit has been a part of this process as I have been relying on him objectively and wholeheartedly. This entire process of being led by God to put together something that is directly from him has been just an absolute hoot and I have been blessed so much to have been a part of it.

I would like to simply ask for you to look on the Scriptures with new eyes and a new heart that longs to know the heart of Christ and the Father who loved us so much to have done what he did for us. This is not just a theory but a true love story of our Creator calling out to his children…and throughout his Word this is the voice I hear…

Please, come to us so we can love you and give you rest. Come to us and be in relation with us so we can be with you now and for eternity. Please accept my Son as a gift offering to you from me. I sent him down to earth so he could show you just how much we love you. He can teach you and be the perfect example for you. And of course, die for you, the ultimate sacrifice for your sins. I raised him from the dead so you would no longer fear death, but be transformed, renewed, and with us forever. We would love to have a relationship with you…because we love you. (God)

God's truth and light are self-evident throughout the words of Christ and his disciples, especially Paul. I truly find and experience absolute joy in my life when I have come across another jewel that was hidden between the lines of God's Word, waiting for me to discover.

Throughout this process of writing this book, it has been a beautiful blessing and a delightful journey of sitting back and just listening for God to lead me, guide me and teach me all that he wants for me to tell the world about. He is trying to reach out to you and touch your heart and your soul. I believe that with all that I am.

Love is a word that has taken on an endless variety of uses and meanings. I "love" my car, my house, my job, my wife, my church. But what does pure and true love really mean?

"This is my commandment: Love each other in the same way I have loved you. Greater love has no one than this: to lay down one's life for one's friends." (Jesus, John 15:12–13)

In the Gospel of John, the word "*light*" is used by Jesus nineteen times as just one way that he describes himself to the world. The word "*love*" is used fifty-three times in John to securely point out the purity of Jesus's purpose for coming into the world. Jesus uses many different words and parables to describe either the truth he is explaining or to describe himself in relation to the world or to us. There is a consistent theme throughout the New Testament which consists of Jesus's true identity and his one glorifying purpose for being here. He is relating, in so many ways, that if you want to get to heaven, then HE is the only way.

"Then he said, 'I tell you the truth, you will see heaven open up and the angels of God ascending and descending on the Son of Man, the one who is the stairway to heaven.'" (Jesus, John 1:51)

"Then midway through the festival, Jesus went up to the Temple and began to teach. The people were surprised when they heard him. 'How does he know so much when he hasn't been trained?' they asked.

"So Jesus told them, 'My message is not my own; it comes from God who sent me. Anyone who wants to do the will of God will know whether my teaching is from God or merely my own. Those who speak for themselves want glory only for themselves, but a person who seeks to honor the one who sent him speaks truth, not lies.'" (Jesus, John 7:14–18)

And the truth will set you free…

"Jesus said to the people who believed in him, 'You are truly my disciples if you remain faithful to my teachings. And you will know the truth and the truth will set you free.'"

The people then replied…

"But we are the descendants of Abraham," they said. "We have never been slaves to anyone. What do you mean, 'You will be set free'?

"Jesus replied, 'I tell you the truth, everyone who sins is a slave to sin. A slave is not a permanent member of the family, but a son is part of the family forever. So if the Son sets you free, you are truly free.'" (John 8:31–36, emphasis mine)

The important message in these verses is relaying that the truth of Christ and the belief in that truth will set you free from the slavery of sin so that you are an inherent and adopted son or daughter into God's Kingdom. That, my friends, is Good News!

One of my greatest joys in this beautiful life is spreading love throughout many different avenues and in as many ways that I possibly can. When Jesus gets ahold of your heart and transforms you, you begin to see the world in so many different shades and colors like never before. Your love for others, for nature, for justice, and equality begins to shine brighter than anything else. The love and light that is growing inside you propels you like a slingshot to move with a purpose of wanting to change lives and love on everyone, especially the lost, the orphans and the needy.

"You are the light of the world—like a city on a hilltop that cannot be hidden. No one lights a lamp and then puts it under a basket. Instead, a lamp is placed on a stand, where it gives light to everyone in the house. In the same way, let your good deeds shine out for all to see, so that everyone will praise your heavenly Father." (Jesus, Matthew 5:14–16)

It is always important to remember that we are to be a light that brings glory to our Father in heaven and not to bring attention to ourselves. This can be tricky because, we as humans, love attention and praise. So keep your focus on God while serving others aiming to give glory to God for the opportunities to love and serve all those that God brings to you.

In our constantly advancing world of technology, war, politics, and greed, there is far too much going on around us that wants to suck the life out of us and basically tear us down to feel hopeless and desperate. I have done my best to view life through a completely different lens. But it always comes down to a choice.

It will continuously amaze me to the degree in which people will focus all their energy, finances and purpose to seek acceptance, praise and supposed security in the negative and sometimes heartless world in which we live.

But again, it is always a choice.

"For we speak as messengers approved by God to be entrusted with the Good News. Our purpose is to please God, not people. He alone examines the motives of our hearts." (Paul, 1 Thessalonians 2:4)

This much I know is true…life is way too short. With the time we are given, and none of us knows for sure how much sand is left in our hour glass, we must look at life through the eyes of a child. Get excited about the little things and don't sweat the small stuff. A house is just a house. And if you have one…be grateful. Stop focusing on always trying to upgrade. Be happy and content with what you have, feel blessed and praise your heavenly Father for such gifts. Choose to use your own time, money and energy to make a difference and change someone's life for the better instead of consistently looking for ways to fill your own life with more stuff.

"But if we are living in the light as God is in the light, then we have fellowship with each other, and the blood of Jesus, his Son, cleanses us from all sin. If we claim we have no sin, we are only fooling ourselves and not living in the truth. But if we confess our sins to him, he is faithful and just to forgive us our sins and to cleanse us from all wickedness. If we claim we have not sinned, we are calling God a liar and showing that his word has no place in our hearts." (1 John 1:7–10)

When I went to Uganda, Africa, for my second mission trip in 2007, I had the wonderful experience of visiting my sponsored family through *World Vision* for the second time. Witnessing *World Vision* in action is an incredibly beautiful sight to see for they are truly legitimate, caring, and trustworthy in serving people all over the world with the love and truth of Jesus Christ.

I even got to see my sponsored child, Godfrey, and his family a second time. Godfrey had made a whole bunch of toys out of mud and clay. He was very creative in his sculpting and designing of all these different kinds of people and animals doing different things and in different poses. It was quite amazing to see. He was generous enough to let me have one of these toys he had made so I picked out the one of a boy doing a handstand. So cool.

In Africa, they hardly have anything. In fact, most people don't even own a mattress, let alone have any clue as to what is actually going on in the rest of the world.

But isn't it interesting to point out that even if something was going on in the world, let's say, something rather epic, they still would probably have no idea about it and it doesn't affect them one bit. Our social media, news outlets and every other form of "news" is not good news, it is usually depressing, disgusting, unnecessary bantering, criticizing, gossiping and slowly dismantling our hope not only in the leaders of our government and in the world but also in the hope of humanity. The stories of death are usually not far behind.

Quite honestly, I have ceased to watch any form of news for years now and I have little to no idea what is going on in the world. Please don't misunderstand me, I keep my ear to the ground and sleep with one eye open, but I am not stepping into the thick muck of malarkey that seems to deeply penetrate the minds and lives of so many people. I have never seen any value in that whatsoever. Negativity to the nth degree!

"Did I offer peace today? Did I bring a smile to someone's face? Did I say words of healing? Did I let go of my anger and resentment? Did I forgive? Did I love? These are the real questions." (Henri Nouwen)

Throughout my life, I have seen by example, a life lived without such drama and no use for news or technology other than the basics. It has become the norm to get sucked into the rapids of the social stream with a sense of urgency to keep up with all the new do-dads and rinky-dinks so as to not look cheap, poor or out of place with an inexpensive flip phone. I would much rather have a flip phone than my so-called smart phone which is really a dumb phone. Quite honestly, I miss my flip phone.

In my perspective, technology is pulling us further away from our quality time with God. Time is being sucked up in all the social media outlets while the billion dollar industry of pornography is killing people slowly, adding to the list of addictions that provide major dysfunction and warped illusions in the minds of young and old alike.

Relationships and marriages are being broken apart because the ease of use and access to internet porn through technology. Are we better off with all our new technology? Are our families benefitting from it or are they being pulled apart? Because of technology there is isolation, addiction to smart phones, addiction to gaming, addiction to internet porn and the problem of being unaware of the world around them. Kids are no longer playing outside, riding bikes, building forts and climbing trees. Not anymore. Kids are becoming less active, unhealthier, and only think about getting home to play video games or be on their phones. It is scary and sad to see the changes taking place. Where do we go from here?

Jesus came into the world to bring light into all the dark places and to reveal truth among the lies. Jesus made many things clear to us and showed us how corrupt our world truly is. Even two thousand years ago, the Pharisees, supposedly the "good guys," were making a mess out of God's plan. Listen here to Jesus explaining how they haven't got a clue.

"'Yes, I realize that you are descendants of Abraham. And yet some of you are trying to kill me because there's no room in your hearts for my message. I am telling you what I saw when I was with my Father. But you are following the advice of your father.'

'Our father is Abraham!' they declared.

"'No,' Jesus replied, 'for if you really were the children of Abraham, you would follow his example. Instead, you are trying to kill me because I told you the truth, which I heard from God, Abraham never did such a thing. No, you are imitating your real father.'

"They replied, 'We aren't illegitimate children! God himself is our true Father.'

"Jesus told them, 'If God were your Father, you would love me, because I have come to you from God. I am not here on my own, but he sent me. Why can't you understand what I am saying? It's because you can't even hear me! For you are the children of your father the devil, and you love to do the evil things he does. He was a murderer from the beginning. He has always hated the truth, because there is no truth in him. When he lies, it is consistent with his character; for he is a liar and the father of lies. So when I tell the truth, you just naturally don't believe me! Which of you can truthfully accuse me of sin? And since I am telling you the truth, why don't you believe me?'

"Anyone who belongs to God listens gladly to the words of God. But you don't listen because you don't belong to God.'" (Jesus, Gospel of John 8:41–47)

The sad truth is this: people are consumed and even addicted to their social status including their material belongings, which in their minds makes them look more important and gives them a false sense of security and a masked identity. It falls right in line with that old bumper sticker that says: *He who dies with the most toys wins!"* How bass-ackward is that?

When Jesus is not the central focal point of your life then I think it is important to ask yourself… What is? Or…who is?

"And so, dear brothers and sisters, I plead with you to give your bodies to God because of all he has done for you. Let them be a living and holy sacrifice—the kind he will find acceptable. This is truly the way to worship him. Do not conform to the pattern of this world, but be transformed by the renewing of your mind. Then you will be able to test and approve what God's will is—his good, pleasing and perfect will." (Paul, Romans 12:1–2)

"Many people did believe in him, however, including some of the Jewish leaders. But they wouldn't admit it for fear that the Pharisees would expel them from the synagogue. For they loved human praise more than the praise of God.

"Jesus shouted to the crowds, 'If you trust me, you are trusting not only me, but also God who sent me. For when you see me, you are seeing the one who sent me. I have come as a light to shine in this dark world, so that all who put their trust in me will no longer remain in the dark. I will not judge those who hear me but don't obey me, for I have come to save the world and not to judge it. But all who reject me and my message will be judged on the day of judgement by the truth I have spoken.'" (John 12:42–48)

I believe the messages from Christ are crystal clear. Either you choose to hear it, believe it and apply to your life or you don't. There is no easy way out, no grey area for you to ease into. You have heard the truth and have seen the light…it is what you do with that information going forward that will determine your final outcome.

Life in all its beauty eventually comes to an end. You hear of it every day. Some of you have experienced a heavy loss in a close family member, a friend or even your own child. Precious is the word I use to describe life in all its fullness. From conception to birth, from a child to an adult and eventually the end of life. It is a cycle that is inevitable. How you choose to live this life is 100 percent up to you. No one else. It all comes down to a choice—your choice.

"If you love me, obey my commandments." (Jesus, John 14:1)

It is really as simple as that. Love him or leave him behind.

I know this truth does not sit well with many but why sugarcoat it? With something as serious and as precious as this very subject is, why would we not take it extremely serious? I don't believe it is a casual decision to make on the fly or to be flippant in how you choose to follow Jesus and obey him. In obeying his commandments…you are loving him. If we disobey him and his commandments then I believe that is the opposite of loving him. Am I wrong? Thank God for his amazing grace.

"And we can be sure that we know him if we obey his commandments. If someone claims 'I know God,' but doesn't obey God's commandments, that person is a liar and is not living in the truth. But those who obey God's word truly show how completely they love him. That is how we know we are living in him. Those who say they live in God should live their lives as Jesus did." (1 John 2:3–6)

Many believe that to obey him is somehow implying that we are then subjecting ourselves and our wills in the direction of slavery. Or that by following Christ your life will be dull and boring. That is clearly not the case or even close to what Jesus is asking us to do. If you look closely at what he is asking…it is crystal clear that his words, direction and commands are far better for us than when we go rogue and try to live life of our own free will and through our own selfish choices.

Just one example of this is my very own life. In my first book, *This Thing Called Life*, I try and give grave details into my personal testimony of failure after failure in my attempts to live life without God at the helm. Choosing to believe that not only am I unworthy of his love and grace, but that I can do just fine on my own. Boy was I completely wrong.

Throughout the story of my life, there is one crazy example after another, ship wreck after ship wreck as I left behind me a wake of destruction and brokenness, sadness, and tears. Poor choice after poor choice.

We all have to eventually "grow up" and face the music. There has to come a time when our incompatibility with God has to change. We cannot allow ourselves to pull out the God card that sits in our back pocket while playing the Monopoly of life, just for those moments when we screw up so we can hand it to God as a way to justify your sins and actions. He will do it for you, though; he will forgive you, if your repentance is sincere. Every single time…because he loves you and his grace is forever. I know this to be true because that is what he has done for me. This wretched and sinful man that I am doesn't deserve the love that Jesus has poured out over me again and again.

But because he has, and I know full well that my sins were many, I cry almost every time when I feel his love and know that he loves me so much as to show me so much mercy and grace upon me and my poor choices. I am shedding tears right now as I am writing these words.

When will each of us come to this amazing truth: that God's love is never ending and his grace is sufficient for our lives? When will each of us, who call ourselves Christians, stop the madness of our secular choices and choose to please God and not ourselves, not the world, but God?

Don't we want so much more than that? Don't you want to know him deeply and relationally? Don't you want to know and feel his love, his light, and his truth penetrate your life so heavily that you have no doubts and no worries? That your life is in his hands and you will be just fine…because you are always in the arms of your

Savior? This…this is what he wants, but you have to let him. There has to come a time in your life where you choose to surrender. And I mean SURRENDER it ALL to the trusting and loving arms of Jesus Christ.

Surrender your bank account, surrender your children, your career, your choices, surrender your marriage, surrender your addictions, surrender your insecurity, surrender your identity and your relationships…surrender it all. Another set of words for surrender is to trust and believe.

We need to quit trying to stay in control of our lives and choose to release control into the trusting hands of God. But this is a task that will require a tremendous shift in your personal choices, a sacrifice in who you once were into who God wants you to be. But I can assure you…it will be the most freeing thing you could ever possibly choose to do.

Before my wife and I started dating, she was in New York and I was in Washington State. I was just starting up my second huge yard sale fundraiser when out of the blue and over Facebook, she contacts me to let me know she wants to sponsor a whole storage unit for the entire six month process until the time of the sale in July of 2016. This was just one more, amongst many, amazing answers to prayer that happened throughout that second yard sale ministry. But what I didn't know was that this donation was the answer to her prayers from God as to where he wanted her tax return tithing to go. This slight encounter in the faithfulness of my then future wife, and unbeknownst to us, was the beginning of our incredible relationship.

We both grew up in the Snoqualmie Valley and had known each other before she left Washington. We went to the same church for a while and were more acquaintances than friends. But after this decision to faithfully sponsor a storage unit, social media connected us more frequently and we started talking a little bit more. As we started talking again, and it had been at least two years since we had even chatted with each other, we realized that neither of us were married any longer and both of us were divorced. Which is sad in itself and a choice neither of us wanted, but ended up being the reality of our lives.

Both of us had chosen to live our lives on the edge and not in the wisdom and commandments of Christ. If we had, there is a far greater chance that we would have not ended up in marriages that were destructive, toxic, and incredibly broken.

As we began the process of catching up with each other, we fell in love. Mind you, we fell in love over the phone and then we fell even deeper in love over Skype. Two months later, I was on my way to New York to give this woman our first kiss. It was very romantic and we were so very blessed. Not long after that, we knew we had to be together. It would be a challenge for that to happen anytime soon, though. She was in the Air National Guard and had committed to a contract job and it didn't look like she would be able to get out of it. On top of the fact that she would also have to sell her house.

Well, as you can assume, we started praying together. And we prayed diligently and purposefully believing that this was a part of God's plan. We didn't know how this would unfold, but we constantly said out loud and claimed it, that we will "trust and believe" that God would open all the doors for us so we could be together and get married.

It was our battle cry for weeks and it was our choice to "trust and believe."

There were a couple more trips to New York and during that time she secured a position part time with the Washington Air National Guard and was released from her job in NY. We put her house on the market and received a full offer within one week. In June, only four months after our first phone call, I flew to New York with two of my three kids (the oldest was in college). With Lena's son, Brock, a cat and a dog, all five of us jumped into an RV and drove across the United States from NY to WA.

We trusted and we believed and God opened every door for us…because he loves us. In August of that same year we were married and it has been a dream come true ever since. This coming August of 2019, we will be married for three years.

My wife and I have worked very hard to make sure that we are putting God first in every detail of our life. Surrendering all to him. Our house is not ours but his. Our money is not ours but his. This book I am writing is not mine but his book…it is for His Glory, not mine. When you surrender, you become less as God becomes more. This is life worth living and it is so incredibly beautiful.

(Side note from Lena, the wife and the editor: We each had to go through LONG periods of releasing control and learning to trust God. Only then did he bring us together. I truly thought I would spend the rest of my life only with Jesus, no husband, and I accepted that. He gave me so much more!)

Sadly, many will be incapable of seeing the fruit and the blessings in this choice of losing one's own life for the sake of Christ and his Kingdom. It will be a choice too hard to let go of. There will be many who will not be able to sever the strings that are attached to so many material things they will deem as more important than choosing Christ. There will be many who will struggle to detach themselves from the world and all that it has to offer. They can't let go of their free will and will continue to live their life as they see fit.

Pride, ego, greed, addictions, envy, and jealousy rise up and take control once again. The only way to battle this disease of the world is to seek out a true relationship with Jesus and begin the process of trusting and believing in the light of the world who is the only Way, the Truth, and the Life.

"Do not love this world nor the things it offers you, for when you love the world, you do not have the love of the Father in you. For the world offers only a craving for physical pleasure, a craving for everything we see, and pride in our achievements and possessions. These are not from the Father, but are from this world. And this world is fading away, along with everything that people crave. But anyone who does what pleases God will live forever." (1 John 2:15–17)

I simply love the light of Jesus and I love his truth. I have found nothing in this world…nothing…that compares to his love and compassion, his mercy and his grace he has shown me time and time again. Humanity never deserved such love, but he gives it to us anyway. And for that, I will be forever in his debt and forever grateful that he allows me to be a part of his family. I have been adopted and so can you. Choose wisely then, for your life in eternity depends on it.

"Don't let your hearts be troubled. Trust in God, and trust also in me. There is more than enough room in my Father's house. If this were not so, would I have told you that I am going to prepare a place for you? When everything is ready, I will come and get you, so that you will always be with me where I am." (Jesus, John 14:1–4)

"For you know quite well that the day of the Lord's return will come unexpectedly, like a thief in the night. When people are saying, 'Everything is peaceful and secure,' then disaster will fall on them as suddenly as a pregnant woman's labor pains begin. And there will be no escape.

"But you aren't in the dark about these things, dear brothers and sisters, and you won't be surprised when the day of the Lord comes like a thief. For you are all children of the light and of the day; we don't belong to darkness and night. So be on your guard, not asleep like the others. Stay alert and be clearheaded. Night is the time when people sleep and drinkers get drunk. But let us who live in the light be clearheaded, protected by the armor of faith and love, and wearing as our helmet the confidence of our salvation.

"For God chose to save us through our Lord Jesus Christ, not to pour out his anger on us. Christ died for us so that, whether we are dead or alive when he returns, we can live with him forever. So encourage each other and build each other up, just as you are already doing." (Paul, 1 Thessalonians 5:2–11)

Chapter 10

Love Never Fails

"Don't just pretend to love others. Really love them. Hate what is wrong. Hold tightly to what is good. Love each other with genuine affection, and take delight in honoring each other."

—Paul, Roman 12:9–10

"Since God chose you to be the holy people, you must clothe yourselves with tenderhearted mercy, kindness, humility, gentleness, and peace. Make allowance for each other's faults, and forgive anyone who offends you. Remember, the Lord forgave you, so you must forgive others. Above all, clothe yourselves with love, which binds us all together in perfect harmony."
—Paul, Colossians 3:12-14

"The Christian does not think God will love us because we are good, but that God will make us good because He loves us."
—C. S. Lewis

Not long after my wife and I were married, we wanted to find a Bible verse that easily sums up our dedication and love that we have for each other in choosing to be married forever, founded in our faith and belief in Jesus Christ...no matter what. After a diligent search, this verse was the winner:

"Love never fails." (Paul, 1 Corinthians 13:8)

Simple but elegant and straight to the point.

We fail sometimes as human beings but love never fails. And even though we fail God, he continues to love us with grace, forgiveness, and mercy.

This truth and analogy is one that many cannot swallow and have a hard time accepting as truth. So far as much as keeping a great divide between the loved and the one who loves. *"How could God love me, a complete mess of a human being, who has done horrible, despicable things to the point that I am extremely ashamed of my life?"* This quote has been repeated many times, from the beginning of time and even now, in the minds of people all across the globe. You may be one of them. I *was* one of them.

Honestly, I don't know if there is a more beautiful truth in all the world than this one truth: Jesus's love for you and for me is a love that never fails. It never gives up, and never backs down. His love is the deepest, most profound love that is available to us all, no matter the circumstance, no matter the story of your life and no matter what you have done.

The sheer beauty of the transformation of love that it brings is one of pure supernatural significance. It is almost unexplainable because of the power that is held in it to the point of seeing lives completely flipped upside down. I have personally seen people whose lives held nothing but destruction, evil, and carnage in their wake but then are transformed into a new and beautiful creation through the love and forgiveness of Jesus Christ. And that, my friends, is absolutely the best news ever! Through Christ there is hope for us all.

"Perhaps the butterfly is proof that you can go through a great deal of darkness yet become something beautiful." (TobyMac Speak Life)

The transformation of the heart and lives because of the love of Jesus Christ is like nothing else on this earth. Those that choose to finally surrender their lives, their sin and their heart to Christ… receive a heart transplant. And they are usually never the same again.

"This means that anyone who belongs to Christ has become a new person. The old life is gone, a new life has begun!" (Paul, 2 Corinthians 5:17)

There have been many times throughout my life when I was given the chance to talk about my relationship with Jesus. And usually, by the time I was done talking, it was not uncommon to find me wiping away tears from my eyes simply because of the pure joy that was overflowing from a heart that had been miraculously transplanted there. My soul is overwhelmed by the magnitude of his saving grace, his truth and the hope that I have been given to know that I will be with him for eternity.

For many who try to understand the message of Christ from the outside looking in, don't be surprised if you struggle with great difficulty in recognizing the truth or understanding the message that is written within the pages of the Bible.

"If the Good News we preach is hidden behind a veil, it is hidden only from people who are perishing. Satan, who is the god of this world, has blinded the minds of those who don't believe. They are unable to see the glorious light of the Good News. They don't understand this message about the glory of Christ, who is the exact likeness of God.

"You see, we don't go around preaching about ourselves. We preach that Jesus Christ is Lord, and we ourselves are your servants for Jesus' sake. For God, who said, 'Let there be light in the darkness,' has made this light shine in our hearts so we could know the glory of God that is seen in the face of Jesus Christ." (Paul, 2 Corinthians 4:3–6)

I can remember early on in my childhood, having gone to church and Sunday school most of my young life, opening up the Bible and being fascinated by God's word from stories of the Creation, Noah, David, and Goliath. I was amazed by the stories of Daniel in the lion's den, the strength of Sampson and the faith of Abraham. The true stories of the Old Testament were interesting and fun to read, but for me, I was always looking for something more relevant, something closer to my heart, something I could chew on. Something that I could bury my feet in, hunker down and connect to with truths that would forever pierce my heart and eventually my soul.

For me, I found what I was looking for in the New Testament. From Matthew to Revelation, I was enamored and in shock by the simplicity of Jesus's words, parables, and the truths that were buried there. But even more important than that was to read and understand what had taken place over two thousand years ago when the Son of God chose to become human…in the flesh.

"He came into the very world he created, but the world did not recognize him. He came to his own people, and even they rejected him. But to all who believed him and accepted him, he gave the right to become children of God. They are reborn— not with a physical birth resulting from human passion or plan, but a birth that comes from God.

"So the Word (Jesus) became human and made his home among us. He was full of unfailing love and faithfulness. And we have seen his glory, the glory of the Father's one and only son. From his abundance we have all received one gracious blessing after another. For the law (Ten Commandments) was given through Moses, but God's unfailing love and faithfulness came through Jesus Christ. No one has ever seen God. But the Unique One, who is himself God, is near to the Father's heart. He has revealed God to us." (John 1:10–14, 16–18, emphasis mine)

The journey of the heart is one that never ends. We should be in a constant mode of searching and sleuthing to find buried treasure in the words of the Bible, in prayer, in the sermons from the pulpit of our pastors and ministers, friends and books, music and movies. We find Jesus in fellowship with other believers but even more so in the mission fields out on the streets, neighborhoods and work places where we can shine the light of Christ through our actions, our love and our pursuit to be the hands and feet of Christ.

"It will be our love, not our opinions, which will be our greatest contribution to the world." (Bob Goff)

If you are pursuing these things…then you are on the right track. We should be, as believers in Christ, hungry for truth and thirsty for more of God's Good News. It should be on our radar to be looking for opportunities to serve others and love on them every chance we get.

I have found on my own journey through life, that we never stop finding gold nuggets of truth, love and wisdom that God longs to share with each and every one of us. He plants them and buries them throughout his Word so we can uncover them and find them with a tenacity that only brings about a reward and excitement as that of a child on Christmas morning.

Grateful is not a big enough word to explain in great detail the impact that Jesus has had on my life. I am thankful beyond words for the love he has poured over me, the patience he has shown me, the wisdom he has taught me and my own deep and personal relationship with him. He is my life and he is my friend.

"Either way, Christ's love controls us. Since we believe that Christ died for all, we also believe that we have all died to our old life. He died for everyone so that those who receive his new life will no longer live for themselves. Instead, they will live for

Christ, who died and was raised for them." (Paul, 2 Corinthians 5:14–15)

Around sixteen years ago, my eyes were opened and my heart flooded with the truth of my life and then I came to a true understanding. That "aha moment" when the clouds had dissipated and I could see clearly that what I wanted most, was to know God more than anything else in this life. I had lived through many attempts of trying to, "do life," on my own terms and going my own way. Failure after failure, heartache after heartache, I finally realized that this was not working out so well for me. So then, I decided, that it was finally time for me to completely hand over my life to Jesus and lay it at the foot of the cross.

I finally surrendered.

That day, as I laid flat on the ground, my face smothered into the rug of my living room floor, with my arms spread out and my face covered in tears, I prayed for God to humble me and I also prayed for his wisdom so I could see the world through his eyes, not mine. I wanted to go deeper into this understanding of who Jesus truly is and what this life is truly all about. I knew deep down that there had to be more. There had to be so much more.

I will never regret the choice I made to follow him or that I prayed to be humbled and asked for his wisdom. God will give you exactly that to which you have asked for, in his timing, and if it is in his will to do so. Jesus warned us to count the cost of choosing to be a disciple. It is a choice that will most certainly rock your boat.

If you have ever tried to go against the grain of anything in this world then you will understand what that means and how that feels. It is the path of heaviest resistance. You will be challenged at every turn, questioned for every choice, repelled and rebuked for your statements of faith and your beliefs that collide with the world's judgments and so-called truths. You will be judged for every action and every word by your peers, your friends, your co-workers and even your own family. And sadly, in many parts of the world, you will be tortured, mocked, beaten, jailed and even killed for your faith and belief in choosing to be a follower of Jesus Christ. (Just recently, only a few days ago, there were bombings in Sri Lanka that killed over three hundred Christians as they sat in their churches praising God.)

Surrendering your life, and that means all of it, to Christ, is truly a sacrificial choice. You are choosing to let go of the world's temptations and all that consumed you and instead faithfully deciding to climb out of the boat and are asking Jesus if you can come and walk on the water with him.

If we choose to surrender to God, laying down our lives and all that consumes us, we have then given permission for God to start the process of chiseling and chipping away at the person you once were into the person he wants you to be. This beautiful transformation is sometimes painful and challenging, to say the least, but it is absolutely worth it.

There will be days when the temptations of the world will be extremely strong and you will want to run away from God. There will be days where you will fall flat on your face, but God's grace, love and forgiveness is so much bigger than your failures and your sins.

God begins to shine his bright and glorious light into the darkest parts of your soul revealing the disease and the decay that needs to be rectified and healed. This is also a painful but necessary part of the transformation, but again, so incredibly rewarding and beautiful.

My solemn belief, though, is that we are on this journey together, a journey to get to the heart and mind of Christ. You are not alone on this journey. We will do this together.

"But it was to us that God revealed these things by his Spirit. For his Spirit searches out everything and shows us God's deep secrets. No one can know a person's thoughts except that person's own spirit, and no one can know God's thoughts except God's own Spirit. And we have received God's Spirit (not the world's spirit), so we can know the wonderful things God has freely given us.

"When we tell you these things, we do not use words that come from human wisdom. Instead, we speak words given to us by the Spirit, using the Spirit's words to explain spiritual truths. But people who aren't spiritual can't receive these truths from God's Spirit. It all sounds foolish to them and they can't understand it, for only those who are spiritual can understand what the Spirit means. Those who are spiritual can evaluate all things, but they themselves cannot be evaluated by others. For, 'Who can know the Lord's thoughts? Who knows enough to teach him?' But we understand these things, for we have the mind of Christ." (Paul, 1 Corinthians 2:10–16)

The Word of God is simply a mystery to those who have not chosen to follow Christ. It all seems like foolishness and a bunch of religious babble. And because it doesn't make sense to them, they choose to harden their hearts against it. They ridicule it, mock it, and claim that it is simply a crutch for those who are weak.

"Deep down though, I believe people want to understand and trust in the Good News of the Bible, believing that it is authentic and genuine. Sadly though, people choose the material world and all it has to offer over the spiritual blessings and the gifts that cannot be seen. Jesus warned us against going down the road more traveled.

"You can enter God's Kingdom only through the narrow gate. The highway to hell is broad, and its gate is wide for many who choose that way. But the gateway to life is very narrow and the road is difficult, and only a few ever find it." (Jesus, Gospel of Matthew 7:13–14)

This is also a scenario that is at war in the hearts of believers alike. Because of our sinful nature, we as followers of Jesus are in a constant battle with the wages of sin and our selfish choices. To have a mind like Christ is to daily separate ourselves from the things of this world that want our attention, capture our thoughts and try to drown out our focus and relationship with our Savior.

We, as true disciples of The Way, have to find that solid ground with which to build our foundations on so we can stand against the wind and the rainstorms of life. Otherwise, life and all that is in it will come crashing down and erode away our faith and dissipate our strength.

Do not ever doubt that the darkness of this world is real and present at all times. Darkness and the evil one wait patiently to attack at any moment, trying to draw you away so that you will not be *present* in the world changing lives and loving those who are lost with the love of Jesus Christ. The devil will use all his tricks to devour us, trick us, and tempt us. And when we fall and fail again, he will use guilt and shame to make us feel useless and unworthy. Do not fall for these lies and trickery.

But we also have to be on guard for our very souls. Jesus has told us, and it is written, to keep watch and stay strong.

"Prove by the way you live that you have repented of your sins and turned to God. Don't just say to each other, 'We're safe, for we are descendants of Abraham. That means nothing, for I tell you, God can create children of Abraham from these very stones. Even now the ax of God's judgement is poised, ready to sever the roots of the trees. Yes, every tree that does not produce good fruit will be chopped down and thrown into the fire." (John the Baptist, Matthew 3:8–10)

"Not everyone who calls out to me, 'Lord! Lord!' Will enter the Kingdom of Heaven. Only those who actually do the will of my Father in heaven will enter. On judgement day many will say to me, 'Lord! Lord!' We prophesied in your name and cast out demons in your name and performed many miracles in your name. But I will reply, 'I never knew you. Get away from me, you who break God's laws.'" (Jesus, Matthew 7:21–23)

No doubt we are taking up arms to fight in a battle of unheard of proportions. This is not for the weak or faint of heart. We must always recognize and remember that our strength comes from him and him only. But we must also remember that the Apostle Paul gladly boasts of his weaknesses because his real goal is for the power of Christ to rest on him. He is well pleased with weakness because he knows that when he is weak, he is made strong through Christ's strength.

"And He has said to me, 'My grace is sufficient for you, for power is perfected in weakness.' Most gladly, therefore, I will rather boast about my weaknesses, so that the power of Christ may dwell in me. Therefore I am well content with weaknesses, with insults, with distresses, with persecutions, with difficulties, for Christ's sake; for when I am weak, then I am strong." (Paul, 2 Corinthians 12:9–10)

The journey and the adventure of choosing a Christ-like life over the demands of being a follower of money, material things, and people-pleasing is one of the most difficult choices you will ever have to make. In faith, you are trusting in him with your life, your finances, your health, and your family…all of it.

It has taken many years for me to come to this understanding and honestly, I still have to let go and let him have control every day. Because he sent his only Son, Jesus, to earth in bodily form as our great sacrifice…we now have a mediator that has bridged the gap between us and our heavenly Father.

"There was a man named Nicodemus, a Jewish religious leader who was a Pharisee. After dark one evening, he came to speak with Jesus. 'Rabbi,' he said, 'we all know that God has sent you to teach us. Your miraculous signs are evident that God is with you.'

"Jesus replied, 'I tell you the truth, unless you are born again, you cannot see the Kingdom of God.'

"What do you mean?' exclaimed Nicodemus. 'How can an old man go back into his mother's womb and be born again?'

"Jesus replied, 'I assure you, no one can enter the Kingdom of God without being born of water and the Spirit. Humans can reproduce only human life, but the Holy Spirit gives birth to spiritual life. So don't be surprised when I say, 'You must be born again.' The wind blows wherever it wants. Just as you can hear the wind but can't tell where it comes from or where it is going, so you can't explain how people are born of the spirit.'"

"How are these things possible?' Nicodemus asked.

"Jesus replied, 'You are a respected Jewish teacher, and yet you don't understand these things? I assure you, we tell you what we know and have seen, and yet you won't believe our testimony. But if you don't believe me when I tell you about earthly things, how can you possibly believe if I tell you about heavenly things? No one has ever gone to heaven and returned. But the Son of Man [Jesus] has come down from heaven.'

"And as Moses lifted up the bronze snake on a pole in the wilderness, so the Son of Man must be lifted up so that everyone who believes in him will have eternal life.'

"For God so loved the world so much that he gave his one and only Son, so that everyone who believes in him will not perish but have eternal life. God sent his Son into the world not to judge the world, but to save the world through him. There is no judgment against anyone who believes in him. But anyone who does not believe in him has already been judged for not believing in God's one and only Son. And the judgment is based on this fact: God's light came into the world, but people loved the darkness more than the light, for their actions were evil. All who do evil hate the light and refuse to go near it for fear their sins will be exposed. But those who do what is right come to the light so others can see that they are doing what God wants." (Jesus, John 3:1–21)

I recently just watched *Disney's* version of the *Charles Dickens* classic, "*A Christmas Carol.*" Each time I watch it, I am awakened to the deep message that lies within its story. Of course there is more than just one message within this classic tale of greed, poverty, selfishness and redemption. But what I didn't catch on to until recently is the horrifying images of ignorance and want.

As the second of three ghosts, the ghost of Christmas present, visits old *Scrooge*, he eventually reveals to him the two decrepit and broken children beneath his robe sitting at his feet, filled with suffering, anguish and absolute despair. The ghost then explains to *Scrooge* that these children are Ignorance and Want. They are the world's children and represent society's abandonment of the poor and the consequences of that abandonment. *Disney's* version of this story shows these children growing up to become a menace to society. One of them living a life of crime and jailed, the other to prostitution and a mental hospital wrapped up in a white, straight jacket.

The depictions have sadly come true to form with regard to our world, our society, our drug problems, greed of every kind, excessive population of jailed inmates and the destruction of our families from generation to generation. Cursing each new family with the sins and poor choices of their fathers and mothers. Continuing the cycle of abuse in the forms of neglect, abandonment, divorce, physical and sexual abuse, belittling, and drug and alcohol addictions.

It is of no surprise to the dilapidation of our society to see such destruction at the hands of loneliness, suicide, drug and alcohol addiction, mental illness, pornography, and homelessness.

This becomes the painful struggle for so many people who are trying to understand their place in the world. Believe it or not...take God out of the equation, a Godless society, and you will see evil at its finest. We are already experiencing the effects of this choice and I fear it will only get worse.

God is not pushing his will on any of us. He gave us free will so that we would freely choose him over what this world and what the god of this world, Satan, has to offer. If you so choose, follow your own way. Choose to be ignorant to the truths, the creation, the love of Jesus who freely chose death and suffering to take *our place* on that wooden beam with ten-inch pieces of metal slammed into his flesh and bone, his wrists and feet for you and for me.

But never forget...he chose you. He chose you to be on this earth. He chose you to be present and alive so that you could fulfill your purpose that he created you for. And so that hopefully, one day, before it is too late, you would open your heart and mind to see that he loves you passionately and wants to be a part of your life...every part, every day.

"In his kindness God called you to share in his eternal glory by means of Christ Jesus. So after you have suffered a little while, he will restore you, support, and strengthen you, and he will place you on a firm foundation. All power to him forever! Amen." (1 Peter 5:10–11)

We are ALL BROKEN. We are all scattered pieces to a puzzle that Jesus wants to start putting back together to make you whole and alive! But you have to believe that HE, is that missing puzzle piece. You have to *choose* what is most important to you. Jesus will complete the puzzle of your life, if you allow him to.

Has the world and all that it has to offer ever fulfilled you and made you feel whole, alive, beautiful and worthy? Has any material thing ever filled in that gaping hole in your chest that so many people try to fill it with? Clothes, cars, homes, girlfriends, boyfriends, sex, drugs, alcohol, toys, money, etc.? Do they ever fill the void? Is it ever enough?

Christians…I am also talking to you! Wake up and search your heart and your life. Don't miss out on the most beautiful relationship you could ever want or hope for. Stay true in your relationship with Jesus. He is not looking for you to accomplish your list of boxes and check them off each day or that you follow through with your Sunday ritual warming up the pew and making sure people see your face. He wants SO MUCH MORE than that. Relationship people…not religion. The WHOLE BIBLE is about our relationship with God and becoming Christ-like. Don't be foolish to think you are free to do whatever your heart desires.

"But the time is coming—indeed it's here now—when true worshipers will worship the Father in spirit and in truth. The Father is looking for those who will worship him that way. For God is Spirit, so those who worship him must worship in spirit and in truth."

"I tell you the truth, those who listen to my message and believe in God who sent me have eternal life. They will never be condemned for their sins, but they have already passed from death into life." (Jesus, John 4:23–24, 5:24)

"Your approval means nothing to me, because I know you do not have God's love within you. For I have come to you in my Father's name, and you have rejected me. Yet if others come in their own name, you gladly welcome them. No wonder you can't believe! For you gladly honor each other, but you don't care about the honor that comes from the one who alone is God." (Jesus, John 5:41–44)

"Carl Jung, the great psychiatrist, once reflected that we are familiar with the words of Jesus, "Whatever you do to the least of my brethren, that, you do unto me." Then Jung asks a probing question: "What if you discovered that the least of the brethren of Jesus, the one who needs your

love the most, the one you can help the most by loving, the one to whom your love will be most meaningful—what if you discovered that this least of the brethren of Jesus…is you?"

*"Then do for yourself what you would do for others. And that wholesome self-love that Jesus enjoined when He said, 'Love your neighbor **as yourself**' might begin with the simple acknowledgement, 'What is the story of my priesthood?' It is the story of an unfaithful person through whom God continues to work! That word is not consoling, it is freeing, especially for those caught up in the oppression of thinking that God can only work through saints. What a word of healing, forgiveness, and comfort it is for many of us Christians who have discovered that we are earthen vessels who fulfill Jesus's prophecy,*

"'I tell you the truth, Peter—this very night, before the rooster crows, you will deny three times that you even know me.'" (Jesus, Matthew 26:34)

"And the Lord is now calling me a second time, affirming me, enabling me, encouraging me, challenging me all the way into the fullness of faith, hope, and love in the power of His Holy Spirit. Ignorant, weak, sinful person that I am, with easy rationalizations for my sinful behavior, I am being told anew in the unmistakable language of love, 'I am with you, I am for you, I am in you. I expect more failure from you than you expect from yourself.'" (Brennan Manning, *The Ragamuffin Gospel*)

If only we would choose to cry out the name of Jesus, instead of choosing the darkness of this world, the hurt and pain that is so often offered instead of love and forgiveness, we would know what love truly feels like. But sadly, in the depths of our sin and pain we unfortunately don't feel worthy enough. Trust me when I say…*Jesus is waiting for you.*

But Ignorance and Want always seem to get in the way. Our selfishness is a constant battle that we will wage war against until our time here is done or Jesus comes back…either one. They are both inevitable truths. Our ignorance to see past our own faults and selfishness, to see clearly how we treat other people. Our ignorance in not taking the time to research and study the Scriptures, the words of life, so that we could become more knowledgeable in our understanding and our relationship with our Savior. To build our faith and come to a true understanding of what it means to follow Christ.

Our want of everything that will make our lives more comfortable, happy, more fulfilling, but never fill that gaping hole. We want it all and will strive at anything to make sure we get what we want. Our want that succeeds and overrules the needs of the less fortunate, the homeless, the starving, the hurting, the hopeless. Our culture has swallowed us up into the lie that "things" will bring us joy, happiness and purpose. Commercial after commercial, advertisement after advertisement, we are bombarded with this useless garbage with millions upon billions of dollars spent all vying for our attention, our money, time, and want. It is simply sad to the extent of what we have become. Rats on a wheel running after who knows what to fill a hole that is dark and empty instead of turning our lives to the one who can give us joy, purpose, love, and forgiveness.

Our lives, our choices and our souls are always teetering and tottering on the edge of our faith and our belief in God the Father and his Son, Jesus Christ. This is a nonnegotiable truth. You can't be "good enough" to make it into heaven. And conversely, you can't simply accept Christ into your heart, call yourself a "Christian," and then choose to live your life however you feel entitled.

"Why is our generation so unhappy? Because there are many choices of temporary substitutes that we use to fill the void that only God can satisfy." (Lei Vallejo)

I am not blind to the challenges of life and all that attracts us to sin and away from Jesus. I am in the same boat as you, wanting to call out to Jesus so I can come and walk on water with him as Peter did, with a faith unwavering. But it is not as simple as that. Faith is believing without seeing.

My life is riddled with pain, sin and hurt that I chose to cause others and myself…but here is the Good News, you are free from all that the past holds over you. Jesus has already forgiven you and now you must choose to forgive yourself. Be set free so that you can learn to accept the love and forgiveness of Christ. He wants to take the burden from you and give you a beautiful and purposeful life. So that your life can then, in turn, give God all the glory.

As you watch *A Christmas Carol*, look closely at the transformation of the heart that explodes inside of *Ebenezer Scrooge*. Yes, he has seen death and has had the life scared out of him from those three ghosts, but something else happens too. He realizes his faults along the way through life, recognizes his sin in the greed of both his dark heart and in his friend *Jacob Marley*, but chooses to then change what is left of his life. It is never too late to start over. It is never too late to make a change. That is the beauty of God's grace. His grace never runs dry, his forgiveness is never-ending. We just have to be willing to want to make a change. To step out in faith and believe.

And to make a choice to leave Ignorance and Want behind and choose a life of servanthood, a life of freedom from the pain of this world and all that it offers…which is nothing but sin and death.

"If you think you've blown God's plan for your life, rest in this: You, my beautiful friend, are not that powerful." (Lisa Bevere)

Trust me when I say this…you will never have lived and have seen the glory of God's face shining with the brightness of the purest love…until you give away to others who are in great need of your gifts. Love those who are loveless, forgive those who don't deserve it and choose to live a life that is beautiful and free from Want and Ignorance. Love never fails and I can guarantee you that Jesus never will either. For God is love and he loves you…yes, even YOU… passionately!

"Whatever is good and perfect comes down to us from God our Father, who created all the lights in the heavens. He never changes or casts a shifting shadow. He chose to give birth to us by giving us his true word. And we, out of all creation, became his prized possession." (James 1:17–18)

"You can't go back and change the beginning but you can start where you are and change the ending." (C. S. Lewis)

"Jesus Christ knows the worst about you. Nonetheless, He is the one who loves you the most." (A. W. Tozer)

"While you complain about your electric bill, there's someone with no home.

While you complain about your job, there's someone praying for a dollar.

While you complain about the food in your pantry, there's someone praying for crumbs.

While you complain about life, there's someone who didn't wake up today.

Your complaints are simply blessings to others. Be grateful and thank God every day!" (Victory Today)

"At the end of life, what really matters is not what we bought but what we built; not what we got but what we shared; not our competence but our character; and not our success, but our significance. Live a life that matters. Live a life of love." (Author unknown)

Chapter 11

No Longer Condemned

"Dearly beloved, we are gathered here today to get through this thing called life. Electric word life, it means forever and that's a mighty long time, but I'm here to tell you...there's something else...the afterworld. A world of never ending happiness...you can always see the sun...day, or night."

—Prince, *Let's Go Crazy*

"Understand this, my dear brothers and sisters: You must all be quick to listen, slow to speak, and slow to get angry. Human anger does not produce the righteousness God desires. So get rid of all the filth and evil in your lives, and humbly accept the word God has planted in your hearts, for it has the power to save your souls.

"But don't just listen to God's word. You must do what it says. Otherwise, you are only fooling yourselves."

—James 1:19–22

"Jesus did not die to give us a religion. He died so that through faith in him we could have an intimate relationship with God."

—Anonymous

For those of you who know me, I have given this life all I got. Even throughout the dark times of my life, and there have been many, I have strived to be a glimmer of light in a world filled with so much pain and darkness. I am far from perfect and have been known, at times, to be a bit obnoxious and overbearing, a little too loud and excitable. I have been flamboyant, goofy, charismatic and full of energy. Too much energy sometimes and I can see how that could be a problem. I know there have been plenty of times when I should have closed my mouth and listened. But instead I chose to speak when I should have just sat there and held someone, in their pain, instead of trying to "fix" them.

Throughout this book, I have tried with intense diligence from my own life experiences and my testimony, to paint a picture of God's pure love for a lost and broken, basically dysfunctional world. We are all a part of its chaos in one form or another. No one is exempt from the mess we have made, or what our grandparents and their grandparents have left behind for us to make sense of. It is truly our responsibility, each of us, in how we choose to impact this world and all those who are around us, in our vicinity or in our own back yards. The time to act is now. Not tomorrow or next week.

As I have freely done, with very little safeguard to my personal life, shared with you my failures, my brokenness and my poor choices. And sadly, most of my life has been a hot mess. Broken, confused, lost, and selfish. I have allowed the addictions in my life to consume me, control me and I made mistakes that took me years to come to terms with. But eventually, I was able to forgive myself and love myself again as I know, wholeheartedly, that Christ has also done for me.

I have tried with so much of who I am to grab ahold of this thing called life, and make it right. To make wise choices, think of others before myself, to live a life that my kids would be proud of and to know that I have made Jesus even more proud of the man I have worked so hard to become. Life though, is full of so many distractions, so many magnets of temptation pulling you in every direction, demanding your attention, demanding that you come just a little bit closer so it can entangle you in its trap.

This is the fight of our lives and it is a continuous attack on our hearts, our faith and our ability to love.

Yes, I have failed miserably, I have failed in almost every part of my life but I have also chosen to stand up and rebuke the belief that I cannot win or that my life is a total loss! I will *not* sit by, curled up in a fetal position, throw out the white flag and surrender to what the world deems as normal and justified. I know, without a doubt, who stands by me and tells me *"I am with you, lets fight this together"*! And if it becomes too much of a burden, and a heavy blow to my life, I know he will take it from me and carry it for me. His name is Jesus and he is my hero, my friend, and the one who has told me over and over again, throughout my darkness and my pain "you are *loved* passionately, you are *forgiven* completely, you are *not* a failure and I will *never* leave your side."

"Peace is not the absence of trouble, but the presence of Christ." (Sheila Walsh)

He is the one who has brought me to tears over and over again, giving me hope, love, encouragement, peace, forgiveness and the willingness to not give up. I shed tears, just now, as I was writing this last paragraph, fully engulfed in the reality and full knowledge of what he has meant to me and has done for me throughout my broken life. It is simply overwhelming to the indelible depths of his love and mercy. I am so incredibly grateful for the life I have been given, so grateful that I am no longer condemned for my past, for my sins, for my poor choices. I have been set free from my bondage and from the pain of my life. And that is simply the greatest news anyone could ever receive. I am blessed beyond words and that is why I am writing this book.

Freedom is a word that carries a heavy meaning but it is lost to most of us who have never really had to ponder it much. Especially if we have been blessed to have been born at a certain time in history or with the proper color of skin pigmentation.

To properly understand the depths of the word freedom we first need to fathom what it means to have been stuck in a position or place with no hope, to be categorized under a particular race or under extreme bondage with no way out of said circumstances. Without going deep into so many areas where this applies, I will simply use it as a metaphor, to explain the best that I can, my own life experiences and ultimate redemption.

Throughout my time here on earth, I have tried diligently to see life as a very positive and rewarding experience, a gift, which has been wrapped up in the beauty, fun, and humor that comes from being human. I try, with a conscious effort, to not take life too seriously because quite honestly, I don't want to miss even one chance to enjoy it. Life, as we all know, is too short. I have also found in my experiences to keep life simple and without too much drama. Early in life though, drama seemed to follow me around like a lost kitten and my life became way too dramatic.

After experiencing many trials and tribulations that left many scars on my wounded heart, I had to purposefully choose to cut out from my life the things of this world I believed were being a hindrance and a burden. I had to make difficult choices to erase people from my life who directly or indirectly chose to inflict pain, who were toxic to my life and basically unhealthy and a distraction to my overall well-being. But these were all necessary choices for my peace of mind and for the protection of my heart.

Once I came to understand my addictions, my bad habits and my weakest points, the things which had become too much of a temptation for me, I did all that I could (and with a ton of hard work), to eventually cut those out of my life. Putting in place the necessary boundaries to keep me safe and greatly enhance my probability of success against that which destroyed me. Now this doesn't mean that the temptations will just go away or that they will never raise their ugly head again, this just means you are acknowledging your poor choices and your weaknesses, choosing to fight against that which controlled you.

"None of my failures in faithfulness have proved terminal. Again and again radical grace has gripped me in the depths of my being, brought me to accept ownership of my infidelities, and led me back to the fifth step of the AA program: 'Acknowledge to God, another human being, and myself the exact nature of my wrongdoing." (Brennan Manning, *The Ragamuffin Gospel*)

As is with most addictions, and through the process of failing, life presents opportunities where we slowly climb out of our mistakes and then sadly we choose to make another one. I have been crushed and overwhelmed by my selfish desires, I have felt helpless to the desires of the flesh. The weight of my sin so heavily wrapped around my neck, suffocating me and whispering in my ear so devilishly, "You are not worthy of God's love or forgiveness." A thought that has been a battle of the mind for far too long.

In my twenties and thirties, just the thought of failure and knowing I had failed God again was so crippling to me, I began to wonder, why do I even try? How do I compete against all of my natural temptations? When was I going to get to the point of understanding that these addictions, this overwhelming sin, was slowly killing me, slowly killing my soul?

In my brokenness, though, and no matter how dark or how deep my sins had taken me, the loving arms of God's grace would somehow reappear, lifting me up once again and enveloping me with a blanket of pure love. Embracing me and convulsing my soul with unadulterated forgiveness. He offered me freedom from the pit of my pain, my sin and my mess. Freedom to fully embrace and capture within my soul the full meaning of this blessing that contains no words to explain it. No condemnation for those who choose Jesus over what the world has to offer.

"All praise to God, the Father of our Lord Jesus Christ. God is our merciful Father and the source of all comfort. He comforts us in all our troubles so that we can comfort others. When they are troubled, we will be able to give them the same comfort God has given us. For the more we suffer for Christ, the more God will shower us with his comfort through Christ." (Paul, 2 Corinthians 1:3–5)

Despite the struggles of life and the crippling effects of our poor choices, beautiful things can emerge from them if we choose to see them in a different light. We have to see them as blessings, not hindrances. We have to picture them as moments of growth not burdens. I am the man I am because of my brokenness.

"Every test in life makes us bitter or better. Every problem comes to break us or make us. The choice is ours, whether we become the victim or the victor. Therefore, don't make the same mistake twice and learn from your mistakes." (Don McCausland)

I cannot begin to explain what God has done through the painful but necessary changes that have completely transformed my life and has helped me to understand more closely the things that breaks the heart of God.

Jesus entered my life and gave me hope while living in a broken and dysfunctional home as a child. Even though I grew into a bitter and rebellious young man, God helped me with the transformation of my heart to grow into a man who longs to be like Jesus and I ended up loving him passionately and wholeheartedly. Because of his patient and graceful mercy, I found a way out of my pain through the forgiveness of those who hurt me. This became my mission. A mission to find truth in the pain, understanding in the chaos, and in the absence of love, I found the willingness to never give up. I was on a mission to find out the truth of who Jesus really is.

The desire has always been there to serve God and to love and serve others with the love he planted there deep in my heart. But when you're extremely cracked and broken from the ones you trusted in the most, your pain eventually seeps in, drips, and sometimes pours out of those cracks and broken pieces. You are then exposed and vulnerable to others with the reality of your situation and the result of your past. And if you are anything like me, your emotions and your pain are then bare for all to see.

We have a tendency to bleed onto others the blood that was bled onto us. But I have Good News for you…Jesus is the caregiver who will take you in and clean up your wounds, sew up your cuts, wipe clean the blood and start the healing and releasing of your pain. Slowly but surely, you heal from the wounds of your past, learn how powerful forgiveness truly is to your heart and to others. You start to fully understand how loved you truly are and that the grace of God is enough. Freedom.

"For freedom Christ has set us free; stand firm therefore, and do not submit again to a yoke of slavery." (Galatians 5:1)

Once you accept Christ, you start to believe you ARE worthy and you are *no longer condemned* for your poor choices or the pain you inflicted on others…the sin you have committed. Your freedom has come, to finally be able to live in the loving and healing arms of Jesus.

"But whenever someone turns to the Lord, the veil is taken away. For the Lord is the Spirit, and wherever the Spirit of the Lord is, there is freedom. So all of us who have had that veil removed can see and reflect the glory of the Lord. And the Lord—who is the Spirit—makes us more and more like him as we are changed into his glorious image." (Paul, 2 Corinthians 3:16–18)

I praise God every day for my recovery. I praise God for reaching down and grabbing my hand many times throughout my life, because I was willing, so he could pull me up out of the darkness and the sewer of my life. I have always believed and was determined that there was something so much better, something so much more that

I could have and be a part of. I also knew one thing for sure…that I was alive, I was loved and I was forgiven!

Just the other day, I was listening to a song as I was driving down the road when in the middle of this song was the word…dead.

I sat there for a moment thinking about that word, dead. When you say it, it almost sounds as much as it means in the pronunciation of the word. Go ahead…try it. Say the word…dead. It sounds as morbid as the word is pronounced. Now try saying…alive…out loud. In its pronunciation, it is a word that clearly sounds exactly like its meaning should sound. Kind of crazy, isn't it?

Our words can easily have a deep impact on our overall life and all its compartments and files, cracks and broken pieces. Words can affect our attitude, our relationships, our behavior and our reactions. Music has this same affect and our choice of music that we listen to is a direct correlation to how we feel about the world, about life and about what we believe in or what we are faithful to.

One of my favorite songs from the eighties was from the group *Foreigner.* "*I want to know what love is*" was a song that penetrated my heart because of how much I had been lacking in love throughout my entire childhood. There were many other songs that had this same effect on my heart and soul. The list is almost endless with regard to love, acceptance, healing and forgiveness. The songs "*Cat's in the Cradle*" and "*The Living Years*" hit me hard when I first heard them so many years ago. The truths within those songs has resonated with me all these years guiding me to be present and listening to the needs of my own children. We have to be open and aware of what it is they need from us and what it is that they want for us to hear, watch, and acknowledge. They want and need our attention and our affection just like we needed when we were that age.

I believe one of our biggest assets *is* our children. Jesus must come first, then the healthiness of your marriage and time with your spouse. Date nights with your spouse is vital to your relationship and your spouses' cup must remain full. But time with our children is also vital to their well-being, happiness, and security. If we do not invest in them, love them, discipline them and spend quality time with them, then what do we expect of them? There is a very good chance they will end up delinquent, unloved, abandoned and unprepared for what life will eventually throw at them.

Just around the corner, there will be many things that will attempt to grab their attention. It is up to us, as parents, to supply them with the tools necessary to succeed so they can fight against the temptation to gravitate toward drugs, alcohol, sex, pornography, and destruction. Give your children time. Listen to them. Love them, guide them…even if it hurts. They need to know that they are loved and are important. And even more importantly, they need to know Jesus.

"And I am certain that God, who began the good work within you, will continue his work until it is finally finished on the day when Christ Jesus returns." (Paul, Philippians 1:6)

As believers in Christ, we don't give up on each other but choose to have grace, love and forgiveness. We have to choose to love each other, even the most lost and brokenhearted. We cannot give up but continue to lean on each other and on the one who will give us the strength we need to go on.

> "Do not be dismayed by the brokenness in the world.
> All things break.
> And all things can be mended.
> Not with time, as they say, but with intention.
> So go. Love intentionally, extravagantly, unconditionally.
> The broken world waits in darkness for the light that is
> you." (L. R. Knost)

I don't know about you, but I want to feel alive, jumping for joy, alive! There is an endless list of blessings all around you. Find them and look for them every day. This might be hard or challenging at first but if we train ourselves, force ourselves to look closely at God's beautiful creation or your good health, or the health of your children, then you will see them more clearly. Choose to see the blessings and acknowledge them.

There are so many people who are struggling to survive. Make a choice to change their lives by your generosity and kindness. Find and seek out ways where your gifts and talents can be used for God's kingdom and to make a difference in the lives of one or many. Give as much as you can for the reward of giving is so amazing. It simply fills my heart when I am able to give in any way that I can.

Let's be real and understand that life will always be challenging. You will still have your good days and a few bad ones, but if you are willing to make a change, grow and do the hard work, God will bless you and the bad days begin to dissipate and the blessings become highlighted and are more apparent. The world becomes brighter, more vibrant and alive. Life in itself becomes more valuable and your purposes become more important.

The simplicity and pure beauty in nature is a wonderful thing to never take for granted. Strive to spend time with God looking at the starry sky or in the glorious sunrise of each new day realizing that *His* creation was made for us to enjoy and to savor. His fingerprints are everywhere from the creatures that walk the earth to the very DNA that is in your blood. He is the Intelligent Designer, the God of the universe, who has truly made it clear as to whom we should glorify. The One who gave us life, breath and an inhabitable planet in which to survive.

Always remember that "Love Never Fails" (1 Corinthians 13:8) and I can personally vouch for that. Jesus has never failed me nor has he ever left my side. We have all sinned and failed in life. We have all fallen short and are sinners at heart. But Jesus took our place on the cross, the one true sacrifice, the spotless Lamb, so we are no longer in fear of death but are looking forward to eternal life. It is time for each of us to take off our masks and accept who we are. Unique, loved, cherished and created by God for his wonderful purpose. Choose to realize that you are beautiful and you are important and God has a plan for your life...a purpose to which He created you for!

"Live a life filled with love, following the example of Christ." (Paul, Ephesians 5:2)

Always remember that our example and how we choose to live life will define us in the eyes of others and they will know you by your fruit. So walk with a purpose, choose your words wisely and give to others without the worry of receiving anything in return.

Give to your heart's content without judgment or worrying about where your gifts will end up being used in the hands of the less fortunate. Let God worry about that.

Never stop searching the Scriptures for truth and the love that is buried there within its pages because the truth will set you free. The Word of God, the Scriptures, will be the brightest light on your path of life. Hold it close to your heart strongly and read it, study it, chew on it. For that is when you will know and understand the life God is asking you to live. Stay strong in your faith. Miracles and healings still take place...you just have to believe that God's plan is better than your own. For Jesus is truth and he is the light of the world. Let the Scriptures transform you, change you and give you a life of purpose, wisdom, and understanding. Freedom is there and within reach for everyone if we so choose to find it.

My life verse is Romans 8:1, which I have touched on throughout this book and at the beginning of this chapter. This was the verse that changed my life. Like me, you are **no longer condemned** for your sins and poor choices if you have accepted Christ into your life and into your heart. This is The Good News...and I believe it is the greatest news that has ever been shared. You have the ultimate freedom in Christ, the hope of which to hang your hat on with absolute, full blown guarantee that this life is not the end. This is only the beginning. Death does not complete the saga. It is not the final say or the sad ending. Jesus changed all of that with his magnificent display of pure love and sacrifice. Evil does not win, Good has already conquered it! Thank you Jesus with all that I am.

I am bringing you Good News! Good News for all who choose to listen and obey!

The Good News is Jesus Christ and the fact that He loves you and me, passionately, completely, and wholeheartedly! He is Life and he is Love! He is my Rock, he is my Teacher, my Hope, my King, my Master and The Holy One. He is my Savior, he is my Light, he is the Chosen One, he is the Author of Life, he is the Guardian of my soul, the Morning Star, Eternal Life, he is my Advocate, he is the Son of God and he is THE MAN!

My hope and prayer for you is that these words, this book, will bring you closer to Christ and that the veil would be pulled away.

If there comes a time, in the near future, when God chooses to tap me on the shoulder once again and says to me, "*Sit down, my son, I have more that needs to be written and shared*"…I will see you then…on the road of life. Always remember and know that I sincerely love you all and pray for those who find this book…that you will be touched deeply by the hand and the love of Jesus.

And finally, I would just like to say one more time, that there is no greater truth, no deeper love you will ever find, than in the blood stained words of the Scriptures. Truly embrace them and let them soak into your very soul…so that they will be written on your hearts and drenched into the very fibers of your being. In them, and in your relationship with Jesus, you will find all of your heart's content and then some. My job here is done. I have given it my best, to bring you, the Good News.

"But the wisdom from above is first of all pure. It is also peace loving, gentle at times, and willing to yield to others. It is full of mercy and good deeds. It shows no favoritism and is always sincere. And those who are peacemakers will plant seeds of peace and reap a harvest of righteousness." (James 3:17–18)

"But you must continue to believe this truth and stand firmly in it. Don't drift away from the assurance you received when you heard the Good News. The Good News has been preached all over the world." (Paul, Colossians 1:23)

Jesus came and told his disciples, "I have been given all authority in heaven and on earth. Therefore, go and make disciples of all the nations, baptizing them in the name of the Father and the Son and the Holy Spirit. Teach these new disciples to obey all the commands I have given you. And be sure of this: I am with you always, even to the end of the age." (Jesus, Matthew 28:18–20)

About the Author

Don Baunsgard lives in North Bend, Washington, with his wife and family. He loves being a school bus driver for his community and is passionate about his faith.

CPSIA information can be obtained
at www.ICGtesting.com
Printed in the USA
JSHW020839191122
33385JS00002B/8